#3

The
Dawn of Motoring

Mercedes-Benz UK Ltd.

CONTENTS

Gottlieb Daimler opened the
doors to motor manufacture
in Britain.
  Cars like his early belt-
driven car (far right) were
built both in Cannstatt and
Coventry.

Introduction

Introduction

Karl Benz (1844-1929) was granted a patent for his design of a car in January 1886.

We take the motor car so much for granted nowadays that it is hardly possible to conceive of a time when it was not with us. Yet 1986 marks only the first hundred years of its being. A hundred years ago, there were no petrol stations or garages, no automobile associations, no Grand Prix racing stars, or any business empires built on the sale of tyres, spark plugs or radio-cassette players for cars – because there were no cars.

This is why the year 1886 is so important in contemporary human history. It was in that year that mankind took its first faltering footsteps towards the age of the motor car. In January, Benz was

granted a patent for his motor vehicle, and a few months later, Daimler installed one of his experimental petrol engines into a 'horseless carriage'.

If we look back to the middle of the last century, we see a Britain at the peak of industrial development and strength. Yet it was on the Continent that the motor car first became established in 1886, and it was to be almost a full decade before it really started to get going in the United Kingdom.

While there had been earlier successful attempts at providing mankind with locomotion, these depended on huge, clumsy and often dangerous steam engines. Indeed, so dangerous were they

The Benz 'Patent Motor Wagen' was first seen running on the streets of Mannheim in June 1886.

that successive British governments passed restrictive laws which hampered the beginning of motorisation in this country. Fortunately, once the door was opened, the British engineer was able to benefit from the experience of his Continental counterparts.

Through a fascinating process of cross-fertilisation, Britain was eventually able to reap the rewards of work started by famous Englishmen such as James Watt and Richard Trevethick. Watt first used the term 'horsepower', and Trevethick showed the way towards locomotion with his steam carriage. It was the pioneering work of men such as these which later

opened up the way for Otto, Daimler, Benz and Maybach to develop the internal combustion engine.

Just before the appearance of the first railways in Britain, there had been a brief flowering of steam-powered road-going vehicles. In 1834, Mr. Hancock started a steam coach called the 'Era', running from Paddington to Regents Park and the City at 6d per head, and carrying fourteen passengers. In 1835, Mr. Church built an Omnibus for forty passengers for a company called the London and Birmingham Steam Carriage Co. But the success of the railway movement drove all such traffic off the roads, sped on their

Gottlieb Daimler (1834-1900) can be called the 'Father of the internal combustion engine'.

In 1886, Daimler installed one of his engines in a coach, thus turning it into a 'horseless carriage'.

Introduction

way by punitive Acts of Parliament.

Nevertheless, once the motor vehicle got going in Britain, it was through the motorisation of public transport that its impact on the general public was first experienced.

Although a Parliamentary Commission of Enquiry sat in 1836 and reported strongly in favour of steam carriages on roads, the famous 'Man with the Red Flag Act' of Parliament was passed in 1865. Four years earlier, a Locomotive Act had limited the weight of steam waggons to twelve tons in order to limit damage to roads and bridges, and had imposed a speed limit of ten miles per hour. The Man with the Red Flag Act was to hold up vehicular development in Britain for many years to follow. The Act stated that each vehicle had to be preceded sixty yards ahead by a man carrying a red flag. This enforced a walking pace, and was intended to warn horse-riders and horse-drawn traffic of the approach of a fearsome 'self-propelled machine'.

The restrictive effect of such legislation on the power of British engineering ingenuity may be seen in the fact that, although engineers were working on combustion and electrical engines at the same time as Daimler, Maybach and Benz, these amounted to nothing. For example Edward Butler patented a motor

Goldsworth Gurney's steam carriage of 1827. Early attempts to motorise public transport were based on steam engines, but steam was short-lived as a means of road transport.

tricycle in 1887 and Professor Ayrton was granted a patent for an electro-tricycle as early as 1882.

So it is to South-Western Germany that we must look for the first steps which were to lead eventually to the motorisation of Britain. At either end of the Neckar Valley – some sixty miles apart – two men worked assiduously through the late 1870's and early 1880's to bring the car into being. They were Gottlieb Daimler and Karl Benz, who have been jointly credited with having almost simultaneously developed the world's first practical motor cars in 1886.

The essential difference between the two great early pioneers was that Daimler was a visionary who dreamed of his engines serving mankind, while Benz only ever wanted to be a car-maker. Each was successful in his own way, Daimler living to see his engines at work in the three elements of land, water and air, while Benz was almost certainly first into the field of manufacturing cars in 1894.

While Daimler died as this century dawned, three years before the epoch-making achievement of the Wright Brothers at Kitty Hawk, he did live to see his engines power a balloon flight and an early motor boat, as well as propel a vehicle. Benz, on the other hand, was entirely taken up with the concept of the motor vehicle. He visualised it as a complete entity, and this is evident from his patent of January 1886 which, in the stilted phraseology of the last century, contains a brilliant description of the principles involved.

Although today past differences have long been forgotten, it is important to realise that both men were rivals in the race to produce the car, and subsequently in the drive to win customers all over Europe. However, in 1926 the firms they started in the late nineteenth century were merged, and the company of Daimler-Benz AG continues to flourish today. There is thus a continuity with the early car, which no other contender for the title of 'Inventor of the Car' can match.

In Britain, the success of Daimler's first Mercedes cars in the early 1900's caused grievous financial losses to the dealers in the Benz marque. Indeed it was to be some years before Benz's fortunes were to recover from the success of the first Mercedes. It certainly caused the failure of some of his early agents in Britain.

Motor buses were a powerful factor in popularising motor transport. This is the first Daimler Cannstatt bus in England, which operated in Helston in 1899.

Introduction

Wilhelm Maybach (1846-1929) was Daimler's collaborator. He is best known as the creator of the Mercedes car.

The earliest cars were frail and spidery, and looked more like carriages than cars. This is the first British-built Daimler, 1896.

The Mercedes car of 1901, created by Wilhelm Maybach, Daimler's collaborator, captured the public imagination, not least because of its euphonious name. The car was so successful that the name stuck, and was later adopted by the Daimler factory as a trade mark. This car more than any other can be said to have dragged the infant motor car kicking and screaming into the twentieth century. Overnight it made the frail and spidery creations of the late nineteenth century, which looked more like carriages without horses than cars, obsolete. With its powerful four-cylinder engine driving the rear wheels through a four-speed gate change gearbox and with its cooling provided by a honeycomb radiator, it became the pattern for conventional car design for many years to come.

It is perhaps interesting to speculate which of the two great automotive pioneers contributed most to the motorisation of Britain. It is a question which can never be properly resolved. Daimler became a strong Anglophile following his early student visit to Britain. Later, he took part in the famous Emancipation Run of 1896. It was thanks to his friendship with the young Englishman, Frederick Simms, that the principle of the internal combustion engine was first demonstrated in Britain in 1891.

Karl Benz almost certainly built the first ever petrol-driven car to run on British soil. Either the 1888 Benz in the Science Museum in London, or the model imported by Henry Hewetson in 1894, must have been Britain's first car.

When it came to the question of popularising the new development, other entrepreneurial spirits come into the story. In Britain the obstacles to be overcome were considerable. It was a time for clever men to show their skill at public relations. The horse still reigned supreme. Government and business were in the hands of the horsey set, aided by a reactionary magistracy which viewed the idea of universal mobility with just as much disfavour as the squirearchy had looked upon the coming of the railways earlier in the nineteenth century.

Men like Frederick Simms, Walter Arnold and Henry Hewetson were to bring the fruits of Daimler and Benz's work to an unwilling Britain, only through considerable self-sacrifice. They believed passionately in their cause, and often broke what they saw as unjust laws in order to achieve their objectives.

The horse dominated until the late nineteenth century. Although the wretched Man with the Red Flag rule had been removed by 1878, right up until 1896 there was still a requirement for a pedestrian to precede a motor vehicle on the public highway, limiting progress to four miles per hour. Motorists were still expected to give way whenever they encountered a horse and rider, which was very often. It was not something they appreciated greatly, given the difficulties of stopping and re-starting.

Simms, Arnold and Hewetson worked tirelessly to change the law, and mounted a brilliant campaign to get the motor car accepted in Britain. In order to achieve their objective, they attracted the interest of the Royal Family, organised motor shows, and even started up a magazine purely for automobile interests.

Their first major achievement was the passing of the Emancipation Act of 1896. This event marked the true start of Britain's motoring history. However, it only removed the preceding pedestrian requirement, and merely lifted the speed limit from a walking pace to twelve mph, where it was to stay until 1903. There was therefore still plenty of work for the pioneers to do.

These three men could be said to have been the founders of the British motor

The first truly modern car was the Mercedes of 1901.

industry and trade. Simms helped to set up the Daimler Motor Company of Coventry, from which sprang the giant that today is the British motor industry. Hewetson and his partner, Walter Arnold, could be said to have been the forerunners of today's indispensable friend of the motorist – the motor trade.

All this grew, however, from the activities of Daimler, Benz and Maybach. It was their genius and stubborn perseverance in the face of many difficulties which was to take man out of the horse age, and enable him eventually to put his wheel tracks on the moon.

Running like a thread through the tireless work of these early pioneers and their collaborators is a striving for perfection. They were never satisfied with their results and were always seeking better ways to solve problems. It was a tradition they were to hand on to their successors at Daimler-Benz AG, charged with the task of developing new products.

Still today, Daimler's motto is writ large on the walls of the Apprentice School in Sindelfingen, where the car workers of the future are trained by Daimler-Benz:

Das Beste oder Nichts
it proclaims – Nothing but the Best.

Rivalry between early motorists and devotees of 'Dobbin' lasted well into the twentieth century.
This early advertisement (far right) shows the wide range of uses for Daimler's engines.

—The Men of Vision—

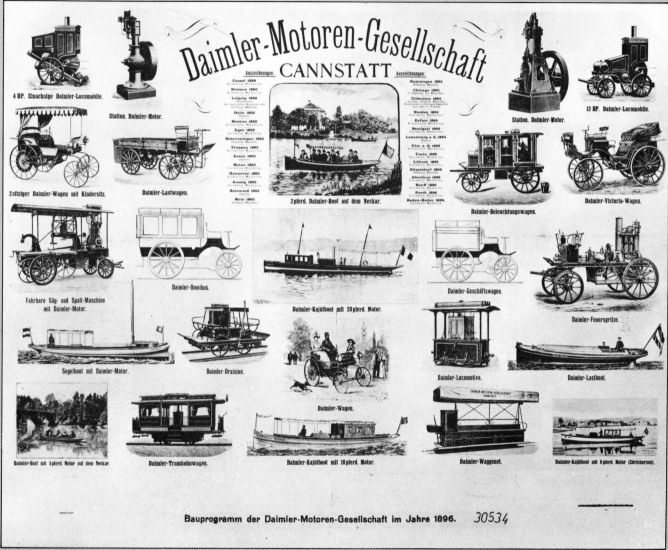

Bauprogramm der Daimler-Motoren-Gesellschaft im Jahre 1896.   30534

The Men of Vision

The entrance to the Great
Exhibition, 1851. The fine
gates were made at
Coalbrookdale, the
birthplace of the modern
British iron industry in the
early eighteenth century.

It is fashionable nowadays to consider man's achievements in terms of the sum of human knowledge. Such knowledge is an unfathomable quantity at best, but in recent times it has been accepted as having increased beyond all measure since the beginning of this century. This may be so, with man having achieved heavier-than-air flight, then supersonic flight, and finally the exploration of space. But the seeds of these achievements were planted in the nineteenth century by such men of vision as Guglielmo Marchese Marconi, Graham Alexander Bell, Gottlieb Daimler, Wilhelm Maybach and Karl Benz.

The nineteenth century was a truly remarkable time. At its beginning, men were still wearing powdered wigs and knee breeches. In 1805, Nelson's ships depended on wind and muscle-power and their cannon threw balls little different, apart from size and weight, from those of Drake and Raleigh centuries earlier. At the end of the century, man had begun to move at a speed faster than that of the fleetest horse.

The industrial revolution which made Britain great can be traced back to the first successful iron casting of the Quaker iron-masters of the seventeenth century. It was their achievements, coupled with that of later engineers such as Isambard Kingdom Brunel, George Stephenson and James Watt, which brought Britain to the pinnacle of industrial success in the mid-nineteenth century. The great mid-century exhibition was held at Crystal Palace to celebrate the nation's prowess.

Although in 1851, England was the richest, most powerful, most industrially sophisticated nation in the world, it was on the Continent, in South-Western Germany to be precise, that the internal combustion engine was to be developed, and flowing from that the motor car. The brief flowering of steam-powered road-going coaches in Britain was nipped in the bud by vested interests in horse transport, notably wealthy landowners who dominated the turnpike trusts. The landowners levied punitive tolls on mechanically propelled road vehicles, and persuaded Parliament to introduce legislation which virtually drove them off the road. As a result, by 1855 most of Britain's considerable engineering and financial talent had been turned to the

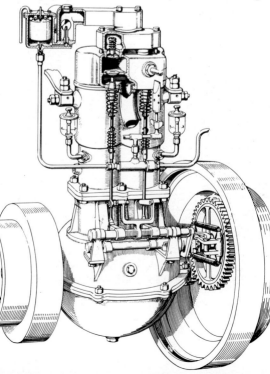

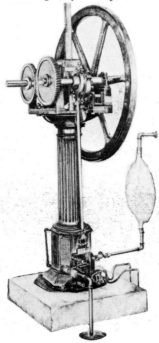

The first atmospheric engine (below) of Otto and Langen (1867) led to Otto's development of the four-stroke principle.

By 1893 Daimler had developed a two-cylinder engine (left) offering smooth running and flexibility.

17

The Men of Vision

Daimler's birthplace in Schorndorf has been restored as a tribute to his memory.

development of the railways.

Four German engineers played a decisive role in the process which was to lead to the development of the motor car. They were Nikolaus August Otto, Gottlieb Daimler, Wilhelm Maybach and Karl Benz. We are here concerned mainly with the last three, but must pay a passing tribute to the genius of Nikolaus August Otto.

Every youngster now knows how a four-stroke engine works, the piston rising and falling in the cylinder, the valves opening and closing to admit the fuel/air mixture and expel it after the explosion which drives the piston down. But the principle had to be discovered first of all, and laid out in engineering terms so that it would work in practice. This was Otto's achievement and no-one can take it from him. Daimler was later to work with Otto in the manufacture of huge stationary town gas engines. But he could see their limitations, and early in his career was dreaming of developing smaller, lighter and faster-running engines able to operate independently of the town gas supply.

Gottlieb Daimler was born in 1834, the son of a baker whose family had served the town of Schorndorf in that role for generations. The young Daimler had always been interested in technical matters, and after serving an apprenticeship with a carbine manufacturer, he came to Britain as a young student engineer. His apprentice piece was a double-barrelled pistol with rifled barrels and nicely chased scrollwork. He lavished the greatest care in its making and was released from his apprenticeship with high praise.

Daimler's family circle in the grounds of his Cannstatt home, 1885.

'Iron and Coal' by William Bell Scott, 1861. This sketch for a mural (far right) expresses the pride in industrial achievement in mid-nineteenth century Britain.

The Men of Vision

Daimler dreamed of his engines serving mankind in the three elements of land, air and water. Left to right: his mobile quadricycle test bench of 1885, the Wolfert airship gondola of 1888 and a test boat run on the River Neckar in 1887.

By the time we see him as a young student in England, in 1861, he is already flirting with the idea of improving on the steam engine. He had spent some time working as the foreman of a locomotive shop, but he was already restless and had decided that the steam engine was not what interested him. He told his employer that what did hold his interest was the problem stated by the Englishman Cheverton in 1826, the need for an engine which would always be ready to start instantly and would not cost too much to run. Later on, other engineers were to devote much attention to speeding up the time it took to set a steam engine into operation, leading to flash-firing of the boiler. But what Daimler's fertile mind was searching for was a smaller, lighter and more manageable engine, capable of being adapted to a number of roles.

Indeed Daimler was something of a visionary. In later years he dreamed of his engine serving mankind on land, water and in the air. He lived to see his dreams fulfilled. His lightweight high speed engine provided the motive power for the first motor vehicle, a crude quadricycle test bench in 1885, the first motor boat of 1886, and the first ever internal combustion-engine-powered flight by a dirigible balloon in 1888.

Years later, his heirs recalled that during a spell away from home he had drawn on a postcard a star over his home, and written that *"one day a star will arise to recognise my work"*. They adopted the three-pointed star symbol, which is still used today as a mark of this realised ambition. It is also generally accepted

that the three points of the star stand for the three elements in which Daimler's engines now work for mankind.

When Daimler arrived in Leeds he was deeply impressed by the power of the industrial revolution at work. He worked for a while in the engine shop of Smith, Peacock and Tannet, before moving on to Manchester where he was employed by Roberts & Co., who made textile machines. He later moved to Coventry where he worked for a time for Whitworths. This company was world famous for its precision work in machine tools and for having created the standard thread dimensions which were used throughout industry.

Daimler chose to visit Coventry because the city was already well established as an industrial centre. For the same reason it

was the logical place for the establishment of his British undertaking many years later, which was to mark the beginning of motor manufacture in the United Kingdom. The setting up of the Daimler Motor Company played an important role in establishing the motor industry in the West Midlands. It was in fact through this early student visit to Britain that Gottlieb Daimler became such a strong Anglophile.

Since railways and locomotive engines were the main direction of engineering thought in the the mid-nineteenth century, it is hardly surprising that both Daimler and Benz were influenced by them. Karl Benz was born in Pfaffenrot in the Black Forest in 1844. His father, Hanns Georg Benz, was an engine driver, who died while Karl was quite small. The

Benz was the first motor manufacturer in the world. His wife Bertha (opposite page) demonstrated the practicability of his invention.

railways were then shaking Europe out of its economic lethargy, and bringing not only communities, but also countries closer together.

The youthful Karl Benz was much taken with mechanical things. His widowed mother gave him a room in the attic where he passed his time repairing Black Forest clocks. Later in his memoirs he was to write of *"the marvellous language that gear wheels talk when they mesh one with another"*.

As a young student, he came under the influence of another then famous, but now largely forgotten, German engineer, Ferdinand Redtenbacher. Later Benz recalled that his teacher felt the steam engine had to be supplemented by something better. He told the young Benz, *"We need to get to the bottom of the problem of heat"*. Once that was done, the steam engine could be thrown away. The key invention must first be made so that engines could be kept down to a reasonable size. The key invention of which Redtenbacher spoke was the internal combustion engine to which his young pupil was later to make such a big contribution. Alas Redtenbacher was not to live to see it, and the young Karl Benz was among the student pallbearers who carried him to his final resting place in the year 1863.

Benz pursued a somewhat chequered business career in which he was strongly supported by his wife's family. He seems to have been on the brink of financial disaster several times, and in the late 1870's was under considerable pressure to make a discovery of vital importance to the economy of the time - a discovery which would also restore his personal financial security. He looked for his salvation in engines and set about studying everything connected with them.

Benz was handicapped in his experimental work in two ways. First, by the existence of the Otto patent of the four-stroke principle, and second, by the crude electrics of the day, since he believed in spark ignition. So in order not to infringe the Otto patent, he had to try to build a two-stroke engine. He persevered with his experiments, and when it first ran, his car had a spark plug and coil ignition, which were the forerunners of those so familiar today.

Benz achieved a first modest success on

Following the merger of the Daimler and the Benz companies in 1926, their symbols were combined.

New Year's Eve 1879. His wife had said to him, *"Let's go over to the shop and try our luck once more"*. Writing later, he recalled:

"My heart was pounding. I turned the crank – the engine started to 'put, put, put' and the music of the future sounded with a regular rhythm in our ears. We both listened to it for a full hour, fascinated, never tiring of its single-toned song. For this New Year's Eve we felt we could dispense with the good wishes of our neighbours. We stood in the courtyard and listened to the 'put, put, put' of the future ....."

Frau Benz had proved an invaluable helpmate and encouragement to her husband. It is said of modern wives that they recharge the batteries of their husbands after a hard day at the office – but she did it literally. She used to sit and treadle away at her sewing machine in the evenings, but she was not sewing – she was driving a small generator which was putting the juice back into the crude early batteries of the time, which were all that her husband had to work with.

Fortunately for Benz he was able to perfect the two-stroke engine to a point where it could be marketed as a stationary power unit. He was then able to devote every spare moment to the creation of a powered car, although his partners were not too keen on the idea and stayed aloof from what they saw as a waste of time. Another stroke of good luck was the granting of a judgment limiting Otto's exclusive rights to the four-stroke principle. Benz was able to take advantage of this, and the fact that the engine was integrated into the totality of his car concept, when he presented his drawings to the patent office.

The path to success was not always smooth. The first trials of the Benz car saw Frau Benz running alongside, clapping her hands in wild enthusiasm. At the next one, she took her place beside her husband and shared his impatience as the engine failed to fire when the flywheel was pulled round. Tensely the driver instructed his assistant. Then with rapid, echoing explosions the carriage leaped forward, completely out of control. After throwing Mr. and Mrs. Benz clear, the vehicle wrecked itself against a wall.

No ceremony marked the next trial, but again the dauntless Frau Benz sat primly alongside her husband while the carriage jerkily moved about a hundred yards before spluttering to a stop. Then came a non-stop run of just over half a mile at a speed of seven and a half miles per hour.

The press were not so easily convinced. The *Mannheimer Zeitung* described Benz's invention as *"useless, ridiculous and indecent"*. It asked: *"Who is interested in such a contrivance as a horseless carriage so long as there are horses for sale?"*

It was Frau Benz who was to demonstrate beyond any shadow of a doubt the future potential for universal transportation of her husband's invention. In the summer of 1888, she undertook an epic journey which was to show to the world that a new age of 'self-mobility' was dawning.

1

3

5

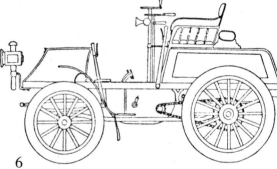

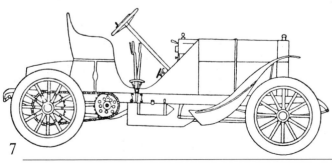

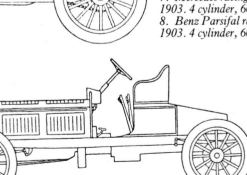

7

2

4

6

8

How Daimler and Benz cars developed.
1. Daimler Steel-wheeled car, 1889. 2 cylinder, 1.65 hp.
2. Benz Victoria car, 1893. 1 cylinder, 5 hp.
3. Daimler Vis-a-Vis, 1894. 2 cylinder, 3.7 hp.
4. Benz Velo, 1894. 1 cylinder, 1.5 hp.
5. Daimler Phoenix racing car, 1889. 4 cylinder, 27 hp.
6. Benz racing car, 1899. 2 cylinder, 12 hp.
7. Mercedes racing car, 1903. 4 cylinder, 60 hp.
8. Benz Parsifal racing car, 1903. 4 cylinder, 60 hp.

The Men of Vision

With her two teenage sons, Eugen (15) and Richard (13½), and without her husband's permission, she decided to take one of his experimental cars for a trip from Mannheim to Pforzheim to visit some relatives. Nowadays it takes the average car driver less than an hour on the Autobahn. But in those days the roads were merely cart tracks and there were, of course, no garages or petrol stations along the way – nor any automobile clubs to turn to in case of trouble.

Early on a fine morning in August, they set out while Papa Benz was still asleep. Eugen drove and, as he later told historian Friedrich Schildberger, they bought

Karl Benz with his family in front of his factory in Mannheim, 1894.
Opposite: By 1911, motoring had become so popular that the Royal Automobile Club was able to open sumptuous new premises in Pall Mall.

petrol from the apothecary in Wiesloch where they also filled the radiator with water. In order to climb the hills, Eugen and his mother had to get out and push for all they were worth while the younger (and lighter) Richard steered. Their comment on the lack of hill-climbing power later led Benz to introduce a multi-speed transmission into his design. In a village called Bauschlott, a cobbler was employed to put a new piece of leather onto the wooden brake block, and they took on more water.

At almost every turn, they must have startled people and horses - it is difficult at this distance of time to judge just what sort of impact they must have had on the rural countryside through which they passed. Other problems were fixed by the boys with some feminine accessories such as a garter and a hatpin. The hatpin was used to clear a blocked fuel jet, and the garter to put some spring back into a faulty electrical circuit.

Their journey took the whole day and fortunately for the adventurers, Papa Benz was not angry when advised of their safe arrival. He merely demanded the return of the chains on the vehicle by fast freight train, as they were needed for an exhibition car which was being prepared for a show in Munich. Frau Benz was rightly proud of her sons' achievement, but history ought to record that this was a time not only of men of vision, but also of women with courage. Frau Benz demonstrated to the world that a new means of transport was at hand.

Birth of the British Motor Industry

Birth of the British Motor Industry

Frederick Simms (1863-1944). Engineer, entrepreneur and inventor, he introduced the petrol engine to Britain in 1891.

Beneath a railway arch at Putney in the suburbs of London may seem an unlikely place for a great industry to be born. But along with Coventry, where the manufacture of the first British built Daimler cars was undertaken, this could be said to have been the cradle of the British motor industry.

It was there in 1891 that a young Englishman, Frederick Simms, set up a business for the importation of engines from the Daimler factory at Bad Cannstatt in Germany.

When it comes to the question of which Englishman had the most to do with the introduction of the internal combustion engine into Britain, Frederick Simms is the obvious candidate. Born of English parents in the city of Hamburg in 1863, Simms was a brilliant businessman. He struck up a chance acquaintance with Gottlieb Daimler when the two met at an exhibition in Bremen in 1890.

Simms was in Bremen to exhibit an aerial cableway which he had designed to provide passenger transport over rivers, valleys etc. A year earlier, he had invented and patented an automatic railway ticket machine, the principle of which is still employed throughout the world. He was therefore not slow to recognise the various fields in which the Daimler engine could be employed.

What particularly interested Simms was the system of Hot Tube Ignition which Daimler had invented to fire up his engine. This used a tube, sealed at one end, running from the outside of the cylinder head into the combustion chamber. It had a device not unlike a bunsen burner fed by its own spirit fuel supply, to play a flame on the outer end of the tube. When this glowed cherry red, the engine was ready to start. What also appealed to Simms' keen engineering mind was that the device was self-timing, and therefore entirely automatic in its action. It needed neither slide nor any other type of valve.

The Hot Tube Ignition brought a new word into being, that of 'chauffeur' from the French word *chauffer*, meaning 'to

An advertisement of 1914 showing the wide variety of livery available for chauffeurs.

heat.' In the early households of the car-owning rich, the man who warmed up the car for his master each day became known as the chauffeur.

Daimler and his collaborator Wilhelm Maybach felt they had found in Simms a young man of uncommon intellect and foresight. They therefore decided to entrust him with the licence to develop the Daimler engine throughout the British Empire, excluding only Canada. Later Simms was appointed to the Board of the Daimler Motoren Gesellschaft, and frequently visited Bad Cannstatt. The business relationship ripened into a close friendship.

But Simms faced enormous difficulties in introducing the Daimler engine into Britain. At first he wanted to bring in an engine fitted to a car, but the difficulties proved too great. Britain was then – and had been for centuries – a very horse-loving country. Anything calculated to oust the 'friend of man' from its pre-eminent position in Victorian society was most unwelcome. There was also concern that the volatile fuel used by the new fangled engine would cause fire and explosion.

Next he tried to arrange for the engine to be used to drive a cocoa and chocolate making machine which was to be demonstrated at a German Exhibition in Earls Court. When the authorities learned that the fuel for the Daimler engine was to be some kind of highly inflammable and explosive spirit, they feared the whole exhibition would be blown sky-high, and therefore refused his application.

The indefatigable Simms then thought of demonstrating the engine in a boat on the Serpentine lake in Hyde Park, but once again he was refused permission on the grounds of risk of fire and explosion. Then he applied to the authorities for permission to demonstrate the motor boat on the lake in the grounds of the old Crystal Palace, but was once again turned down.

In the end, Simms had to turn to Old Father Thames. So it was in the summer of 1891 that the internal combustion engine principle first came to Britain in a motor boat, which made a number of demonstration runs between Charing Cross and Westminster Piers.

Later that year Simms rented an arch adjoining Putney Bridge station from the District Railway Co. at a cost of £25 per annum. This few feet of space, used exclusively to fit Daimler engines into boats, might well deserve a blue plaque one day as the birthplace of the motor industry in Britain.

To a considerable extent, Simms' difficulties in demonstrating the internal combustion engine principle in Britain mirror those of Daimler in his early experiments. The *Cannstatter Zeitung* bitterly attacked Daimler in 1885 following the first experimental runs of his quad-ricycle mobile test bed. It talked of the vehicle as being *"repugnant, diabolical and dangerous to the life and well being of the citizens,"* and called for the drastic intervention of the police.

Birth of the British Motor Industry

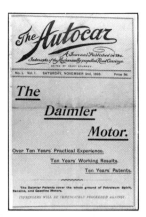

Daimler therefore turned his attention to the installation of his engine in the world's first internal combustion powered motor boat, *The Marie*, which he fitted with a 1½ horse power petrol engine. When he carried out trials on the river Neckar, he disguised the boat with wires and insulators and suggested that it was electrically powered. It was only later, when the psychological battle had been won that he returned to road transport, and installed his engine in a four-seater coach.

For the next five years, Simms was to work diligently to try to remove the obstacles in the way of the motorisation of Britain. Together with his associates, he set about a systematic campaign to explain to the public the advantages of the motor car. It was a campaign which would do justice to a modern public relations case history. To try to get the law amended, they founded a magazine in 1895 – *The Autocar* – which is still published today.

The campaign was led by Sir David Salomons, Mayor of Tunbridge Wells; the Hon. Evelyn Ellis, a member of the De Walden family; Henry Hewetson, a London tea merchant; H.J. Lawson, Simms himself and J.H. Knight from Farnham, Surrey.

In June 1895 Simms and Ellis brought a Panhard & Levassor car with a Daimler engine to England, and drove it in spite of the law from the coast to Ellis' house near Windsor. Ellis, who was very interested in mechanical things had bought a fire engine driven by a Daimler motor as well. Sir David Salomons, a very influential man and a competent engineer, who, like Simms, could foresee a great future for the horseless carriage, had also imported a Peugeot car with a Daimler single-cylinder engine. At that time the number of vehicles in England could be counted on the fingers of just one hand.

In order to inform the public about these vehicles, Sir David Salomons, Simms and Ellis organized an exhibition and demonstration in Tunbridge Wells on October 15th, 1895. A large crowd watched the four cars, three of which were powered by Daimler engines. Later, Sir David Salomons founded the Self-Propelled Traffic Association.

On a Wednesday in December 1895, *The Autocar* reported on what must almost certainly be the first ever car launch in Britain. Simms had just imported one of Daimler's Cannstatt – built belt-driven cars. He invited a number of journalists and other well-known people to a private demonstration. The party was first entertained to lunch in the Garden Restaurant at Crystal Palace, and Simms used the opportunity to enlist the aid of his audience in supporting the Act to be brought before the next meeting of Parliament. It would remove the *"absurd restriction which at present prevented enter-prise in autocar manufacture."* In staging this operation, Simms showed the way to every subsequent motor manufacturer how to get the Press on their side. In other words, he offered a synthesis of hard news together with some hospitality and a personal experience.

It is clear too that he used his close connection with Daimler and his membership of the Board of the Daimler Motoren Gesellschaft of Cannstatt to good effect in staging his company's display at the first ever motor show in Britain, held at the Imperial Institute in London from 9th May to 8th August 1896. The official catalogue shows that the recently formed Daimler Motor Company Ltd of Coventry had on show the original Daimler experimental quadricycle of 1885 and the first Daimler 'motor coach' of 1886 - two priceless exhibits by any standard.

Members of both Houses of Parliament were invited, as were a number of influential people whose support was being solicited for a change in the law. As the exhibition was taking place on private property, it was possible to stage live demonstrations of the new sensation, the 'horseless carriage.'

Even the Queen's eldest son, His Royal Highness the Prince of Wales, later King Edward VII, expressed interest in the novelty of the motor car. He was driven in a belt-driven Daimler car by Frederick Simms, and expressed his enthusiasm for this new means of transport.

Thanks to these campaigning efforts,

The cover of the first issue of 'The Autocar', published a year before cars were free to drive on the roads of Britain.

The exhibition and demonstration held in Tunbridge Wells in October 1895. The Hon. Evelyn Ellis at the tiller.

Birth of the British Motor Industry

Scenes from the Emancipation Run of 14th November 1896 – a 'Red Letter Day' for British motoring. Right: Benz' agents in Britain, Henry Hewetson and Walter Arnold at the start. Opposite above: Henry J. Lawson with his wife. Opposite below: The procession passing along Northumberland Avenue. Opposite right: Cars driving through Reigate. Cyclists joined in too. Below: the menu card for the celebratory dinner.

Saturday, November 4th, 1896.

MENU

THE MOTOR CAR CLUB

DINNER

IN CELEBRATION OF THE PASSING OF THE

LOCOMOTIVES ON HIGHWAYS ACT, 1896,

THE "MAGNA CHARTA" OF MOTOR CARS.

FIRST MOTOR CAR TOUR LONDON TO BRIGHTON,

Birth of the British Motor Industry

Parliament finally enacted a new law not long after the show closed, on 14th November 1896. The Light (Road) Locomotives Act opened the door to the motorisation of Britain, raising the speed limit to twelve miles per hour, and removing the preceding pedestrian rule.

To celebrate this notable victory, the newly formed British Motor Car Club, staged an informal drive from London to Brighton. Some fifty-eight vehicles were entered, of which thirty-five set out from Northumberland Avenue. Before the start, the Earl of Winchelsea solemnly tore up a symbolic red flag. A total of twenty-two vehicles arrived safely in Brighton.

This event, known as the 'Emancipation Run,' is still commemorated on the first Sunday of November each year. It does not seem to have been terribly well organised, in that no proper records were kept. Nevertheless, for those who arrived, there was a celebratory dinner at the Hotel Metropole in Brighton at which speeches were given about the dawning of a new age of automobilism. The tradition of a formal celebratory dinner is still observed by the RAC as part of the London to Brighton run each year.

The Autocar celebrated with an issue printed in red ink under the headline: 'A Red Letter Day.' This is how the magazine reported the story:

"Today, November 14th, 1896 is a red-letter day, not only in the history of automobilism, but in that of England itself, for it marks the throwing open of the highwayes and byeways of our beautiful country to those who elect to travel thereupon in carriages propelled by motors, instead of horse-drawn vehicles or upon bicycles .....

.... Yesterday we were criminals if we ventured out upon the Queen's highways and our journeys were either taken surreptitiously, in fear and trembling as trespassers upon forbidden ground, at the mercy of every country bumpkin in the uniform of the Police force who sought to score points for promotion by securing a "case" or else we rode, where every other British subject enjoyed the right of way, only by the special favour of certain more enlightened authorities.... Today the users of the autocar enjoy the free rights of British citizenship ..... Yesterday the proverbially blind eyes of Justice refused to see anything but an ugly, unwieldy, smoking, puffing traction road engine when an autocar passed by, whilst today, the bandage removed, that good lady recognizes in the same vehicle a light handy carriage, travelling anywhere with the ease and facility of a cycle, but with little noise, no smoke and minimum of other objectionable features....."

Seven days later, the magazine was reporting the Brighton Run in the following terms:

Liberty Day
The Autocar Ride to Brighton

"Great preparations had been made for the event, and the Central Hall in Holborn had been taken over by the Motor Car Club for the purpose of a store house in which the machines coming from the Continent and the country could be safely housed upon their

arrival in London. Here over a score were to be found on Friday evening, and some enthusiasts were so eager to feel their new fledged wings that as soon as the chimes of midnight had passed, and November 14th had legally commenced, they took their cars out for a spin along almost deserted streets. London had risen to the occasion and the crowds were such that the mounted police had to back their mounts into the crowd to make room for the cars to start."

The report goes on to describe how the police were unable to control the crowds so that several breaks occurred in the procession. It added: *"The roads were filthy, and the cars progressed through a deep sea of mud, over surfaces of the most sodden and heavy going character."*

Several of the participants were forced to drop out and continue their journey by train, including the drivers of several electric cars whose accumulators did not have enough power for the whole trip.

Gottlieb Daimler also took part, driving in a barouche of his own manufacture, with Frederick Simms by his side. This was surely a measure of his support for the motoring movement in Britain. This support was also expressed in the great man's willingness to give his name and to serve as a director of the Daimler Motor Company of Coventry, which had been formed a year earlier in 1895.

The mainspring behind this company was Henry J. Lawson, who had been associated with the early days of the cycle movement, and had become wealthy through his dealings in the cycle world. Together with Simms and Henry Sturmey, Editor of *The Autocar*, Lawson became one of the leading members of the campaign to legalise motoring in Britain.

He arranged to purchase the licence for the Daimler patents from Simms, and floated a company called the British Motor Syndicate Ltd. on 21st November 1895 with a capital of £150,000. This was a bold stroke indeed when it is considered that at this time the speed limit for all horseless carriages was still four miles per

Shareholders of the Daimler Motor Company Ltd. in front of the factory building in Coventry, 1897.

hour, and a pedestrian was legally bound to walk in front!

The Autocar diligently reported that same month, under the headline 'Autocars to be manufactured in England' that with absolute certainty all legal restrictions would be removed, and that it was expected that before long there would be a movement to introduce the vehicle commercially into Britain.

Immediately afterwards, Lawson's British Motor Syndicate Ltd. floated off a new company called the Daimler Motor Company Ltd., to manufacture engines and cars bearing the name of 'Daimler' in England, This company was registered on 14th January 1896 with a capital of £100,000 of which sum no less than £40,000 was paid to the British Motor Syndicate Ltd., for rights to manufacture under the Daimler patents. Gottlieb Daimler was appointed a Director, and Simms became Consulting Engineer.

There then followed a brief period when there were two versions of the same Daimler car available – the 'Cannstatt Daimler' and the 'Coventry Daimler', with the British one being a duplicate of the German. Soon, however, Gottlieb Daimler realised that Lawson's real drive was toward money-making rather than experimentation and improvement of the principle, and so he resigned from the Board of Directors. The British company then began to develop its own designs and before long there was a four-cylinder Coventry Daimler in production which owed little or nothing to the German

design.

Later, largely through having been demonstrated to King Edward VII, the British Daimler became a firm favourite of the British Royal Family. Daimler's name together with Simms' entrepreneurial spirit were therefore to be remembered long after they ceased active participation in the Coventry-based firm.

Other entrepreneurial spirits were also at work in Britain at this time, as can be seen from the fact that at the same time that he acquired the Daimler Patents, Lawson also bought out those of the Pennington syndicate. Mr. Pennington, of whom little is known, also took part in the famous London to Brighton Run, naturally in a machine bearing his name. It is described in *The Autocar* as a four-seater tricycle, which was reported to have *"got lost at the start,"* and had to join the procession at a later point because of the press of the crowd.

The brooding genius of George Lanchester was also at work, but he was unable to find the proper backing. The first British production cars, Wolseleys and Lanchesters, did not make their appearance until the turn of the century.

But is is to Frederick Simms that the greatest credit must go for getting the British motor industry started. He also managed to concern himself with the welfare of motorists and the organisation of the budding motor industry and trade. In 1897 he founded the Automobile Club of Great Britain and Ireland, which was later given Royal status in 1907. Five

King Edward VII and Queen Alexandra arriving at Versailles, February 1907, in their 'much discussed' Mercedes, according to the 'Illustrated London News'.

Birth of the British Motor Industry

years later, in 1902, he started the Society of Motor Manufacturers and Traders, having carefully thought up and registered the name in advance. Indeed how he came to bring the SMMT into being provides a fascinating insight into this talented and determined man.

As part of the PR campaign to win approval for the new invention of the motor car, the Automobile Club had staged a Motor Show at Richmond in 1899. The show was a success in every way except financial, and the Club lost some £1,600. Simms therefore decided that what was necessary was a society, to which all manufacturers belonged, that could put on its own exhibitions.

The victory in the Gordon Bennett Cup Race by S.F. Edge in 1902 provided the opportunity that Simms needed to get all the manufacturers and traders together. He invited a number of them to a lunch at the Cecil Hotel in the Strand, ostensibly to celebrate this great racing victory. However, after lunch the guests found themselves rubber-stamping Mr. Simms' latest baby – the Society of Motor Manufacturers and Traders Ltd. – and within an hour were attending the first general meeting of the Society.

They learned that its name had been registered earlier that month as a limited guarantee company, with the principal aim of encouraging and promoting the interests of the motor industry. Another key aim was to ensure that there would be only one major annual motor show rather than a multiplicity of them around the country throughout the year. Simms felt that there should be solidarity on this point, and wanted to create in effect a monopoly of motor shows in Britain. That he was able to achieve this in a manner which lasted for some seventy-five years is a measure of the man. It took the formation of the European Common Market and an outbreak of legislation designed to protect consumers against monopolies, to change the basis upon which the SMMT was formed.

Simms continued to take a keen interest in motor industry affairs until he died in 1944, aged eighty-three.

Motoring was just as much a matter of life-style in 1912 as it is today, judging from this early Lanchester advertisement.

Opposite page: One of Maybach's most successful designs was the 60 hp Mercedes of 1903. This example won nearly all the cups in the foreground at Brooklands.

Maybach
Creator of Mercedes

Maybach – Creator of Mercedes

It was Emil Jellinek who convinced Maybach that road-holding must be improved to cope with more powerful engines.

Doctors were one of the first professions to see the advantages of the car.

As the movement towards motorisation got under way, it was the rich international elite, the leisured classes who first took up driving. To a very considerable extent, the car was the plaything of the rich, although middle-class professional people such as doctors were quick to recognise the advantages it could offer.

So it was perhaps hardly surprising that it was on the newly-discovered French Riviera, that the car first began to be sold commercially. Daimler's agent in France was the dashing Austro-Hungarian consul in Nice, Emil Jellinek. Since Jellinek lived in great style and had good connections with international financial circles and the aristocracy, he soon found distinguished buyers for the Daimler cars which he imported.

The French passion for motor racing did much to develop the reliability of the car, and Jellinek was quick to discover the publicity advantages to be gained from success in motor sport. In 1899 he entered a twenty-three horsepower Cannstatt Daimler in the Nice Speed Week under the pseudonym 'Monsieur Mercedes,' after the name of his favourite daughter, then only nine years of age.

His success was eclipsed shortly after by Panhard and Levassor with their Daimler Phoenix engines in the Paris to Bordeaux race. To add to that, a works driver named Wilhelm Bauer was killed in a Cannstatt Daimler during the race over the mountain course at Nice La Turbie in 1900.

This led Jellinek to maintain that the car needed a brand new concept if it was to be able to handle the greater power which was demanded. He therefore called on Wilhelm Maybach, Daimler's collaborator, to produce a design with a lower centre of gravity and a longer wheelbase so that it could cope with the increased power. The result was Maybach's masterpiece, the Daimler Simplex of 1901.

Maybach's engineering skill and knowledge was fundamental to Daimler's success. He is the 'unsung hero' of those pioneering days, and known to some as the 'king of designers.'

Daimler's collaborator – as Maybach will always be known – first came into the great inventor's life in a rather unusual way. Daimler was working as technical director of the Bruderhaus Engineering Works in Reutlingen in 1867. This was a charitable institution based on Christian

principles, the profits of the enterprise being used to carry on the work of the organisation. One of the orphans cared for by this institution was Wilhelm Maybach. He attracted Daimler's attention because he combined a passion for engineering with creative fervour. In other words, he was that unique blend – a practical man of ideas.

In later years Maybach wrote about his years in the Bruderhaus (meaning 'brother house'):

"After the untimely death of my father and mother when I was ten years old, I went to that well-known friend of orphan children,

Father Werner in the Bruderhaus in Reutlingen. When I was fifteen, I went into apprenticeship, and because I was good at drawing, my job was in the drawing room of the Bruderhaus Engineering Works. I went to evening classes in the town high school where I learned physics and freehand drawing, and at the end of my apprenticeship I was allowed to take the mathematical courses at the city technical college. Around 1867 Daimler was put in charge of the Engineering Works. Two years later he became factory manager for a machine building company in Karlsruhe. He got me a job there in the designing room."

Thus began an association which was to prove not only fruitful in terms of achievement, but also a life-long friendship. Maybach's ability to be self-taught, which he demonstrated in his youth, clearly aided his later work.

In 1867 that other great engineer, Nikolaus August Otto, had developed his famous atmospheric engine, which was the first successful internal combustion engine. When he re-organized his company in the early 1870's into the Gas Motoren Fabrik Deutz in order to manufacture the engine, it was Daimler who was appointed factory manager.

Daimler brought in Maybach as Chief Designer, and together they were successful in bringing the Otto atmospheric engine to a relatively high state of design and quality. Indeed they brought it as far as it could be taken, since it was not capable of any further development. The engine developed only three horse-power

Mercedes Jellinek, the name that launched a famous marque.

Competitors in the Nice 'touring competition' in May 1899 included Emil Jellinek who entered under the pseudonym 'Monsieur Mercedes'.

Maybach – Creator of Mercedes

Maybach first came to Daimler's attention as an orphan at the Bruderhaus in Reutlingen.

Together, Maybach and Daimler built this experimental engine in 1883.

and yet it was of huge weight and bulk. Its sheer size made it virtually of no use to small concerns at all. Otto continued to experiment, and in May 1876 he made what can now be seen as a critical break-through when he set down for the first time the four-stroke cycle. Daimler and Maybach worked together with Otto in the development of a production version, which set the company solidly on the road to success. At the same time they brought about the dawn of modern technology, since they ushered in the age of the internal combustion engine.

This is not to say that all their problems were at an end – far from it. The engines continued to be big and heavy, and they depended on town gas for fuel. So they could only ever be used in a stationary capacity – as power sources for industry

for example. Ignition remained a problem. Otto's four-stroke engine used an ingenious method of igniting the fuel mixture inside the cylinder head by means of a continuously burning flame, which was exposed when needed by a slide valve. But as compression was increased and higher revolutions were sought in the search for more power, the complexity of the system proved somewhat troublesome.

Ignition was to continue to be a difficulty for Daimler and Maybach well after they embarked on their independent course. Since Daimler had a very lucrative contract with Deutz and some savings, together with the dividends he continued to earn from his stockholding in the Deutz company, he was able to resign in 1881 and to set up on his own as a freelance 'inventor.' He moved with his family to Bad Cannstatt, now a suburb of Stuttgart, and set up a workshop there. He enlarged a greenhouse in the garden, and used the toolshed as an office and workshop.

It speaks volumes for Maybach's faith in his mentor that he sacrificed his secure job at Deutz, and readily agreed to join Daimler in Cannstatt. On 18th April 1882, a contract was drawn up between them setting up the relationship which was to start on 1st January 1883. The first clause was:

"Maybach is to take the position as engineer and designer with Daimler in Cannstatt to work out and execute various projects and problems in mechanics as Daimler shall

direct, as well as to perform other technical and business duties for him.''

Their main aim now was to develop a lighter, faster-running engine, which would be able to operate from fuel that it could carry around.

During that first year their efforts were to be crowned with certain success, and Daimler was granted a patent for the 'Daimler motor' on 16th December 1883. The primary feature of this patent concerns the self-ignition of the fuel/air mixture. This was to be achieved by rapid compression of the mixture, which was then to be ignited via a thin-walled tube closed off at one end and projecting into the cylinder. This was kept red-hot by a burner, which played a flame continuously on the exposed end. At first, it was envisaged that this would be necessary only to start the engine which, when hot, would continue to self-ignite. However, it became obvious that the burner had to operate continuously and when this procedure was adopted, the way was opened to development of the high speed engine.

Some idea of the difficulties which had to be overcome before this relatively simple device could be made to work reliably can be gained from a note Daimler wrote some years later:

''It was a long road requiring endless tests and unremitting pursuit of the objective by an experienced engineer, to move ahead from the initially quite hopeless results of work with free ignition. Premature firing of the mixture occurred again and again when the

engine was being started and during compression before (the piston) reached dead centre. Then the flywheel would be suddenly and unexpectedly thrown backwards instead of forwards, and the crank would be ripped right out of the experimental assistant's hand like a bolt of lightning. This made it look as if self-ignition was a practical impossibility until persistent new tests, changes in the shape and size of the combustion chamber, changing the proportions of the mixture, etc. finally brought acceptable and later excellent combustion.''

Seen in terms of today's highly sophisticated breakless transistorised ignition systems, the Daimler hot tube seems crude. Yet it was the second breakthrough following Otto's four-stroke cycle, which was to prove decisive in the achievement of self-mobility for mankind. It used creative engineering to bypass the weak state of electrics at that

The greenhouse of Daimler's house in Bad Cannstatt, where Maybach and Daimler built the first successful lightweight petrol engines.

Maybach – Creator of Mercedes

Maybach is best remembered for having produced the first Mercedes for Jellinek in 1901, seen (far right below) after its famous Nice victory. His virtuosity as a designer made itself felt with his spray carburettor in 1893 (below). He was responsible for the design and production of a whole series of superbly successful sports and racing cars, starting with the 60 hp which won the Gordon Bennett Cup in 1903, the first international motor race to be held in the British Isles. The driver was Jenatzy (right). Further successes came in the Grand Prix races started by the French in 1906.

time, a problem which was to plague his rival, Benz, for many years. It was not until Robert Bosch succeeded in making a low-voltage induction ignition system reliable that Daimler abandoned his hot tube in favour of electricity. This was more than a decade later in 1897. Bosch was also later still to develop high voltage ignition which brought independence from what were still, in 1902, very inadequate and inefficient batteries.

When in order to ensure good sales, Emil Jellinek needed to win back the leadership in the field of motor racing from Panhard and Levassor, it was to Maybach that he turned for a new design. Daimler's health had begun to deteriorate in the middle of 1899.

Jellinek was delighted with the Daimler Simplex, and immediately ordered thirty-six cars. He was granted the agency for Austria-Hungary, France, Belgium and America – an unbelievable franchise territory in today's terms. He also demanded and won the right to market the car in those countries under the name 'Mercedes.' Elsewhere it would be called the 'New Daimler.' The car was so successful on account of its brilliant design and execution that the name Mercedes became firmly established, and was later adopted by the Daimler factory as its marque. Many years later, when the two firms Daimler and Benz were merged, the products became known as 'Mercedes-Benz'.

Another key development which was largely the work of Maybach was that of the spray carburettor. It is the basis of modern carburettor design, and allows the driver to regulate the amount of fuel and air fed into the engine so as to be able to cope with varying loads. This is something we take for granted today, but in the very early days of motoring, things were different. Control was effected by a centrifugal governor. Until Maybach invented the carburettor, when the car was stationary or running slowly, there would first be a cannonade from the exhaust, then a silence as the governor cut in, then another cannonade, and so on.

In the years immediately following Daimler's death in 1900, Maybach continued to work for the Daimler Motoren Gesellschaft and developed further great designs such as the 60 horsepower car which won the Gordon Bennett Race in Ireland in 1903, and the 90 horsepower cars of 1903-04. Later he started a whole new series with the 70 horsepower six-cylinder model. However, with Daimler gone he did not feel any close bond with the management of the company, and felt that he was not given proper credit for these achievements. So on 1st April, 1907, Maybach left the Daimler Motoren Gesellschaft. His great services to technology, were amply recognised during the evening of his life. Medals, titles, and an Honorary Doctorate from the Stuttgart Institute of Technology were heaped on him. He was to live almost ten years into this century, and therefore was able to see for himself the far-reaching effects of his and Daimler's life work.

The Car Arrives in England

The Car Arrives in England

Previous page: cars profited from the cycling boom in late Victorian England, and initially, the two pastimes had much in common.

The car made its appearance at the Paris Exhibition of 1889 (below), just a hundred years after the French Revolution. The French were quick to grasp the advantages of the car, and opened the way to international trade.

Right: Possibly Britain's first car – The Roger Benz of 1888.

The truth of how and when the 1888 Roger Benz car, which is in the possession of the Science Museum in Kensington, came to Britain will probably never be known. The chances are, however, that this was Britain's first car. In other words, it was imported long before the Mannheim-produced Benz made its first appearance here in 1894.

The far-sighted Benz looked beyond the borders of his native Germany to try to win support for the idea of motoring. The French were early enthusiasts. Both Daimler and Benz exhibited at the Paris World Fair of 1889, that extravagant celebration of the centenary of the French Revolution, which gave the world the 1,000-foot Eiffel Tower.

Benz was represented in France by his agent Emile Roger, who showed a three-wheel petrol-engined car, powered by a Benz engine. It was virtually a copy of the Benz Patent Motor Car of 1886, but its three horsepower engine was more powerful. Also instead of the wire spoke wheels and solid rubber tyres of the first design, it had wooden rims and iron tyres.

The car had been purchased by Roger and declared as being of French manufacture, so that it could be entered in the exhibition. In fact, Roger was granted a licence by Benz to build his car from kits of parts supplied from his Mannheim factory. Thus, at a time when Toulouse-Lautrec was capturing the spirit of the fast-changing scene for posterity, motor-making became an international business.

The records of the Science Museum show that they acquired the car in 1913 for the sum of £5. They had been approached by a Miss E.B. Bath of Kings Lynn, Norfolk. A minute in the archives, signed by Mr. E.A. Forword, and dated 8th May 1913, states:

"The car came into the possession of Miss Bath from her brother, a motor engineer, who probably took it in exchange, but at present nothing more is known of its history. It is, of course, not possible to say with certainty when it came into this country, but I should be inclined to the idea that it was ordered by someone who saw the Roger car at Paris in 1889. It may even have been imported by Roger himself in order to exploit the cars in this country. In any case it is highly probable that it was the first petrol

motor car to be imported, and there is little doubt that it is the earliest petrol car we are likely to have an opportunity of acquiring. I have no hesitation, therefore, in recommending that the car be purchased for the sum of £5."

In another minute, dated 24th April 1913, Mr. Forword writes to his Director, Mr. Parkinson that:

"This car is a valuable historical relic and I regard it as a great find. It is one of the three-wheeled French-made Benz cars which preceded the four-wheeled type introduced about 1894 of which we recently obtained a specimen. It is the direct successor of the Benz tricycle of 1885 and specimens must be very rare indeed. I should not have thought it possible to obtain one anywhere, and am very surprised to find one in this country. Mr. Roger, of Paris, was the French licensee of Benz' cars, and he either built the cars to Benz' designs, or simply assembled the parts obtained from the Benz factory at Mannheim..... The work of Karl Benz in the development of the modern motor car was as important, equal in fact to that of Daimler himself, and we should be fully justified in acquiring an example of his first type of vehicle in addition to the later four-wheeled type. (Munich Museum possesses his first tricycle and one of the 3hp cars of 1898). The car should of course be inspected either at Kings Lynn or brought here on approval. The price of £5 would be reasonable."

Determined to secure his Director's approval for the deal, the indefatigable Mr. Forword cites *The Scientific American*

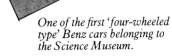

One of the first 'four-wheeled type' Benz cars belonging to the Science Museum.

of 5th January 1889 which published a picture and description taken from a German newspaper, showing a Benz car running in a Munich street at the time of the Exhibition of 1888. *"This car is exactly like the one now offered to us"* he wrote, *"so that the design if not the actual car made by Mr Roger, dates back to 1888 at least."*

Benz's concept of a motor vehicle was a complete one, and this is enshrined in his patent of 29th January 1886. His ideas can be clearly seen in the accompanying drawing, which shows the engine under the seat driving the rear axle through a system of belts, and the single front wheel with its bicycle forks steering system. The wording of the patent application is also very precise: *"A vehicle operated by a gas engine .... whose gas is generated from vaporizable substances by an apparatus carried on the vehicle."*

But it was probably the very completeness of this concept which was to prove a trap. In a way, Benz was a victim of his own early success. He persevered with horizontal rear-mounted engines driving through a system of belts for too long – well into the twentieth century. It was some years before Benz's fortunes were to recover from the success of 'the Mercedes Era.' Maybach's outstanding design was to prove ruinous to Benz's agents in Britain.

The first of these was Henry Hewetson, a tea trader and proprietor of a large milling and general engineering business in Paddock Wood, near Tunbridge Wells in Kent. Hewetson recalled his first

The Car Arrives in England

encounters with a Benz car in a brochure edited by Lord Montagu under the headline *How the Benz came to England*. He was on a visit to Mannheim where one of his friends owned a Benz. He was so impressed by it that he immediately went to Benz and Co. and ordered a two-seater three horsepower model which cost him about £80. Hewetson was struck by the fact that a great gulf had opened up between the Continent and the island state of Britain. On the Continent, the car could be used without hindrance, while in Britain it was subject to many unfair rules. This made him determined to fight for the same sort of rights as those enjoyed by Continental motorists.

Hewetson soon infected his business partner and friend Walter Arnold with his enthusiasm. Hewetson's business had been founded by Arnold's father, William Arnold, under the name William Arnold & Sons. So arrangements were quickly made for Hewetson to become the English concessionaire for Benz cars in association with Walter Arnold. This was in late 1894 and early 1895, just about the time when Simms was beginning to develop the Daimler licence.

Hewetson's action marks the first stirrings of the motor business in Britain. He realised the great potential ahead of the motor car, but he and Arnold had to fight the prejudices against the car existing at that time. To do this, they had to link up with their rival, Simms.

In 1895, Arnold and Simms took some cars to take part in the Battle of Flowers at Eastbourne as part of their campaign to popularise the new means of transport. It was to prove a somewhat salutary lesson on the prejudices of those days.

In Simms' car, the two young daughters of the director of the local gas works sat holding reins attached to the front of the car. An old horse had been hired to take part in the procession with a blanket thrown over it with the letters RIP clearly printed. In addition, the man leading the horse had a wreath with 'In Loving Memory' clearly visible. Not the best possible taste, perhaps. But Arnold and his colleagues were astonished at the adverse reaction of the crowd to this harmless joke. The spectators, angry at this awkward defamation of Dobbin, threw stones mixed in with the confetti with which the procession was being pelted. Arnold was hit in the face and almost disabled.

The two partners, Hewetson and Arnold, began to trade from Hewetson's address in Mark Lane, London, under the title The Arnold Motor Carriage Company. It was under this title that they exhibited at the motor exhibition held at the Imperial Institute in 1896 which was

This illustration (left) accompanied a report in 'The Scientific American' of 5th January 1889.
Above: Henry Hewetson, Benz's first agent in Britain.

The drawings which accompanied Benz's patent application show the completeness of his concept of the car.

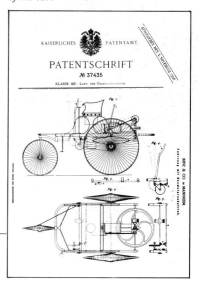

The Battle of the Flowers, held in Eastbourne in 1895 was part of the early joint campaign on behalf of the motorcar.

organised as part of the campaign on behalf of the car.

Walter Arnold, being of a technical turn of mind, decided to follow the example of Roger in Paris, and to start manufacturing Benz cars under licence at his engineering works at Paddock Wood. It may seem remarkable, but the cars made by Arnold under the name Arnold Oil Carriages did not disturb the relationship between Hewetson and Arnold, and Hewetson continued to import and sell fully built-up cars from the Benz works in Mannheim.

Once the new law of 1896 took effect, several Benz cars were sold in Britain as well as a few made by Walter Arnold under licence. Certainly a number of Benz and Arnold cars took part in the Emancipation Run of November 1896, although it seems they may not have

taken part 'officially'. That is to say, they did not start from London. It looks as if one or two Arnold cars went in procession from Walter Arnold's factory in Paddock Wood, and drove directly to Brighton without having troubled to check in at the start! Hewetson and Arnold also took part themselves.

They then decided to re-christen their business Hewetson's Motor Car Company, and it continued as such until 1898, when in view of the large number of Benz cars being sold, it was decided to form a new company called Hewetsons Limited with a total capital of £25,000 in £1 shares. The new company was registered in October 1899 with offices off Oxford Street, W.1. To a certain extent, this business can be said to have been the forerunner of the '... and traders' aspect of Simms' Society of Motor Manufacturers and Traders.

In 1899, the newly formed Automobile Club staged a show and demonstration of motor vehicles of all kinds in the Old Deer Park, Richmond, with hill-climbing and reliability trials. Hewetson entered a twin-cylinder Benz dog cart and a single-cylinder Benz Ideal, both of which were awarded a silver medal. Later Lord Northcliffe's popular daily newspaper *The Daily Mail* offered a prize for a car which could cover one hundred miles without a stop, and a Benz car collected this also.

It is interesting to look at the rivalry which characterised the early days of the commercial activities of Daimler and Benz, which spilled over into their international operations. To a certain extent, the followers of the Benz concept were forced by the success of the first Mercedes to fight aggressively to hold on to their share of the market. Attack being the best form of defence, they responded in an uninhibited fashion to the Daimler challenge. Free from the constraints which apply to today's advertisers, those early combatants on the motor industry scene set about each other with gusto. Take for example the way that Hewetson tried to pull the rug out from under Simms' Daimler:

"*WARNING. Beware of cars with high speed engines, even if water cooled. Our engines run at about 500 rpm and their life is practically everlasting. Engines running at 1,500 rpm or over have a short life – very short – while they cause excessive vibration*

A contemporary illustration underlining the 'fun' aspect of early motoring. A scene from the Automobile Club Show at Richmond, 1899.

An early commercial application of the car was this light van operated by the Benz agents, Hewetsons.

HEWETSON'S LIMITED.
Sole British Agents for
BENZ & Co. Mannheim.
BENZ MOTORS
Offices & Show Rooms.
6 & 7, DEAN St. OXFORD St.
London W.

The Car Arrives in England

Lord Northcliffe (right) was an important figure in promoting the cause of the motor car. He helped to finance the Thousand Mile Trial held in 1900 to bring the car to the attention of people living away from London. The event also demonstrated the reliability of the new means of transport. Right: cars leaving Calcot Park. Opposite page: the conclusion on 12th May. Inset: a scene in Sheffield.

E. J. Coles. Trick driving was an attraction at shows as well as at music halls.

and noise."

As the century drew towards its close, the motor trade gradually became more firmly established. We are indebted to *The Autocar* for a charming report of how a new model Benz came to their attention in March 1899. Compared with the bally-hoo which today surrounds the introduction of a new model, the rather mannered tone seems downright unsophisticated:

The 1899 Benz Car

"Hearing that Messrs. Benz' latest production had made its appearance in London we took the opportunity of a spare hour last week to look up Mr. Hewetson, and found him up to his eyes in business, but not too busy to accord us that courtesy which is one of his characteristics, and he very readily acceded to our wish to try the new pattern vehicle, and we were soon – with Mr. Coles in charge – gaily motoring away in the direction of Hornsey Rise. The new vehicle ran with very little noise and with an extremely small amount of vibration: indeed the improvement in these two respects over the earlier Benz cars which made their appearance in this country is remarkable ...... On Saturday Mr. Hewetson arranged a hill-climbing contest in the neighbourhood of Guildford, and we learn from several correspondents that no difficulty was encountered at any of the rises met with, among the slopes being surmounted being The Mount, Guildford, this with a full load of three, and White Down Hill between Abinger and Effingham, Surrey."

Strenuous efforts still had to be made to demonstrate the reliability and ease of running of the new machines. In 1900, the Automobile Club held its famous Thousand Mile Trial. At this time there were still tens of thousands of people in Britain who had never seen a motor car, and this trial was to show them what a car was like and what it could be expected to do. It would also give the designers something to think about since their products would be subjected to severe tests which had never before been attempted. The trial spanned the last days of April and the first two weeks of May, and the route ran from London to Edinburgh and back.

There were also official hill-climbing tests along the way, including the notorious Shap Fell in Cumbria. Three single-cylinder belt-driven Benz cars were entered for this trial, two in the section for manufacturers or their agents. They were driven by Hewetson and E.J. Coles who had acquired something of a reputation as a trick driver. Coles had also appeared on music hall stages, driving up and down steps, and even steering with his bare toes on the tiller!

The third car was entered by a friend of Hewetson, Mrs. Bazalgette, in the section for privately owned cars, thus demonstrating the ease with which the car could be managed even by a woman. Nowadays this would be judged a sexist remark, but in Queen Victoria's day, women were not expected to take on technically difficult tasks like driving cars – this was to come much later on. Nevertheless Mrs. Bazalgette was to complete the trial and collect a silver medal, a remarkable demonstration by any standards. Although she failed to maintain the average of twelve mph on some sections of the course, she otherwise had no difficulties.

Following the success of the Thousand Mile Trial, many small Benz cars were sold and Hewetsons had to move to larger premises at 251, Tottenham Court Road. But this development took place just as the first Mercedes cars were making their appearance on the scene. The motoring public now began to ask itself whether horizontal engines at the rear, driving through a system of belts were quite the thing, in the light of more powerful vertical engines mounted in front, with gear drive, clutch, etc.- The Mercedes car captured the public imagination because of its reliability and competition successes, and a car such as the Benz which had only a maximum speed of twenty-five mph was rapidly going out of date. Indeed not until four decades later was the rear engine to re-emerge with any conspicious success in the form of the Volkswagen 'Beetle.'

The Thousand Mile Trial had proved that the high speed engine did not 'knock itself to pieces' within a few miles as Hewetsons advertisements claimed. Engines in front had proved satisfactory and even pneumatic tyres had shown that they had great possibilities. Hewetsons were now fighting an uphill battle on behalf of the Benz car which was rapidly becoming out of date. It was for the

purpose of showing the reliability of the Benz principles, that during the summer of 1902, Henry Hewetson undertook to drive a 4½ horsepower belt-driven Benz with a horizontal engine at the rear, a hundred miles per day for three months. He successfully completed the daunting task, but the long trial failed to have the desired effect. Horizontal engines and belt drive were doomed, and the business which Hewetson had built up went steadily downhill from 1903 onwards. During September 1905 the company ceased trading altogether.

An effort was made in 1909 to revive interest in England with the launch of a new company. But this too was doomed to fail, despite the muscular Blitzen Benz taking a world speed record at the newly-opened Brooklands track near Weybridge, Surrey.

The 200 horsepower Blitzen Benz demonstrates how far the car had come in the first decade of this century. Its world record at Brooklands of 127.4 mph is a staggering achievement in the light of the relative youth of the car at this time. It went on to raise its own record to 131.1 mph in Daytona Bay, Florida in 1910, and still further to 141.7 in 1911.

Compare this with the speeds achieved in the first reliability trial of July 1894 over the seventy-five miles from Paris to Rouen, which could be said to have been the world's first motor race. Emile Roger won an award driving a Benz Vis-a-Vis. The average speed was ten and a half mph – well below the speeds of which the

The Car Arrives in England

The drama of record-breaking around high speed tracks such as Brooklands was a powerful influence. Top: the 1911 Blitzen Benz. Below: Resta driving over 103 mph in a Mercedes 1903. Right: Miss Muriel Thompson winning a Ladies' Handicap.

cyclists of the time were capable.

Although Benz made a considerable impact on the start-up of motoring in Britain, his agents were to succumb to the success of the first Mercedes. But his name lives on in the merged company title of Daimler-Benz AG and in the product title of Mercedes-Benz.

—A Time of Change—

A Time of Change

As well as a stout topcoat, a scarf to hold the hat in place was essential wear for the motoring woman of fashion.

With the car came a whole new set of survival problems for the new and more mobile section of society who could afford to use it. At the leisurely pace of the horse, and with enclosed carriages used for long-distance journeys, the mid-to-late nineteenth century traveller had no need of special protective clothing. But the early cars were spartan affairs with little in the way of weather protection. For the most part they were designed as open carriages in order to keep their weight down. So keeping warm and dry became a major consideration.

A report in *The Autocar* in 1901 sets the fashion scene very well:

"When we looked in at Mr Chas Base's tailoring establishment a few days ago we were shown a number of motor garments for winter wear having several noteworthy improvements. Among other novelties is a motor sack or apron made of melton, and lined entirely with fur.

Exteriorily, in the lap of the sack is a fur muff, and below a couple of pockets most conveniently placed. This warm covering is designed sack fashion for gentlemen, being drawn up over the legs; the one for ladies is open down one side, with a series of silk cord loops and buttons easily manipulated to keep it in position when put on. Another noteworthy article of clothing is a handsome fur overcoat made of racoon fur, and lined with tweed, which would defy the keenest wind."

Needless to say, with no windshields or covers, driving in wet weather was miserable, and yachting clothes were often brought into play. The motorist therefore needed protection against rain, dust, heat and snow.

An advertisement in *The Autocar* of January 1902 spoke of the *"Ayrshire Motorcoat, of thoughtful design, able to be used sitting down, with the skirt providing protection for the knees."* Ladies autocoats were trimmed with fur, scarfs were used to hold hats in place and special storm cuffs kept out the wind. Goggles kept eyes safe against the windstream and dust.

Special footwear was not long in coming along either, with Auto-Boots being advertised at seventy shillings the pair, and combined boots with gaiters for better protection. Ladies boots trimmed with fur were only thirty shillings.

The way in which people had to dress up for motoring is entertainingly described in a letter written the same year:

"My wife suggested a drive. I put on a pair of shooting stockings and a pair of field boots, a pair of Dunhill's fur foot coverings, a Russian ponyskin coat, a cap with the ears turned down, goggles, and scarcely any part of my face was left bare: a pair of old dancing gloves of elk calf completed my costume. A fur rug leaving my feet free for the pedals, kept my knees warm. I came home warmer than I started. All through this cold weather I find that the motor is the warmest place except bed."

Goggles were especially important, since many roads were very dusty and drivers often complained of the pain caused by dust in their eyes. Following the passing of the Emancipation Act of

1896, there had been an upsurge in the demand for motor vehicles. Motorists joined the already vociferous cycling lobby in their demands for improved roads, as the existing ones were far from adequate for the new means of transport. Not only were they very dusty or muddy, but often they had no proper foundations. There were many steep hills, and bends were very sharp.

It is perhaps hardly surprising that the roads had fallen into such decay, since the coming of the railways in the earlier part of the nineteenth century took much traffic away from them. In the mid-to-late century therefore, a whole generation grew up to whom the roads were simply peaceful byways.

With the collapse of the turnpike trusts, the rural roads reverted to the old system of parish maintenance, and this meant that any new pressure group had to approach a great number of authorities. In 1850 there were 15,000 separate bodies in England and Wales in charge of the abandoned highways. Eventually, legislation culminated in the Local Government Act of 1888 which brought into being the County Councils, to whom responsibility for the main rural roads passed.

Until the coming of the railways, the King's Highway was busy with horse-drawn traffic. Stage coaches connected the main centres of life with a frequency which now seems surprising. For example, in 1839, twenty-three coaches left Brighton for London every day.

The coaches had, of course, played a significant part in the building up of a road infrastructure in Britain. The period of the greatest road building activity was from 1790 to 1810. It was associated with John Macadam, who gave his name to metalled road surfaces, and with Thomas Telford. The progress in road building reduced the time for coach journeys between key cities. Between 1750 and 1830, for example, the journey from London to Edinburgh was reduced from twelve days to forty-five hours.

But the coming of the railways spelled disaster for the horse-drawn transport business. All over the country, stage coach companies, livery stables, waggoners, carters and coaching inns fell on hard times. The turnpike trusts went bankrupt for lack of customers and for lack of

Goggles were essential wear on the dusty roads of the early 1900's. Drinking and driving does not seem to have been such a problem then.

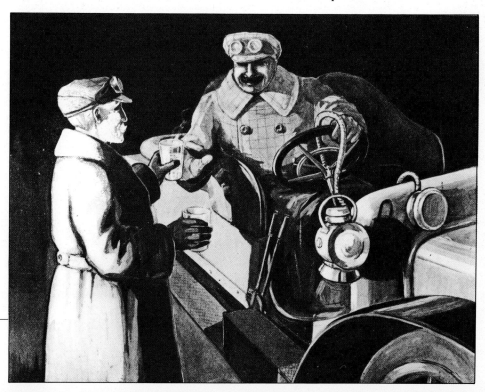

A Time of Change

Practical advice was given to women on how to look after their cars. An illustration from Dorothy Levitt: 'The Woman and the Car', 1906.

funds, and the roads crumbled into soft dusty tracks.

This is not to say that the coaching companies did not put up a spirited fight against the railways. Today's motorists still benefit from a cutting carved through the Chiltern Hills on the A.5, just north of Dunstable, at a cost of £25,000 to the coaching firms. The cutting was intended to try to reduce the time taken by coaches on their journeys north from the capital, but it was doomed to failure.

So when the motor car came upon the scene there was no central administration for roads, and it was possible to find a twenty-mile stretch of road administered by ten separate authorities. In 1902, following two or three years of agitation, the Roads Improvement Association managed to bring about an enquiry into the administration of roads. It was held that bad roads were bad for industrial efficiency, and many towns had inadequate thoroughfares.

Roads had to be made dustless, smooth and watertight for the new vehicles. They also had to withstand the pressure of car tyres. The new rubber tyres, especially those which had studs, caused damage to the old roads. But it was very expensive to improve roads, and County Councils did not possess large funds. Only in 1909 was a Road Board established, whose purpose was to give money to councils for road improvements.

Alongside the development of motoring, there grew up another infant, destined to become a giant world-wide industry. Petroleum had been known to exist as a mineral resource for some time. Its first uses were for illumination and as a cleaning agent.

Britain played a vitally important role in the development of the world-wide petroleum industry. As early as 1794, an Englishman, Robert Street, registered a patent visualising the burning of a liquid fuel such as tar, turpentine or petroleum to move a piston.

The dream fuel, a liquid capable of being carried upon a vehicle which it would then power by being turned into an explodable gas, came into being also in Britain. In 1850 a Scottish chemist, Dr James Young, invented a process for obtaining paraffin from bituminous shales by slow distillation.

In 1859 the first successful drilling of a well for petroleum was carried out in Pennsylvania, USA, and the first oil rush took place. At the same time, a middle-aged chemist named Eugene Carless set up as a distiller and refiner of mineral oils in Hackney Wick, London. In 1872 John Hare Leonard bought Mr. Carless' business and thus came into being Carless, Capel & Leonard. The great contribution of the Leonards, Messrs. William and Charles, John Hare's sons, was to offer

Automobile Association Scouts were an important source of help to early motorists. It was the AA which set up the first roadside filling station in Britain.

63

A Time of Change

In 1901 Carless Capel & Leonard mounted a campaign to explain petrol to 'autocarists'. They published a small booklet (below: the sixth edition of June, 1906) which included prices, a history of petrol, regulations, information on different oils and a list of agents. Right: an advertisement of 1905 shows the uses of petrol in a variety of vehicles.

better fuels.

By the time Frederick Simms met Gottlieb Daimler in 1890, a start had been made in the development of various motor spirits on the Continent. But in England, where cars with internal combustion engines did not yet exist, no suitable spirits were available.

The lack of suitable spirit of high volatility led Frederick Simms to contact Carless, Capel & Leonard as a leading business in the English oil distilling trade. By September of 1891, Simms & Company had begun to take regular deliveries of what Carless, Capel & Leonard described as Launch Spirit at five gallons a time. This was for use in the Daimler internal combustion engine-powered launches which Simms was by then building in his Putney premises.

The association between the two companies continued to flourish and led eventually to the coining of the word 'Petrol'. The entirely logical word Petrol seems to have been the product of Simms' fertile brain. We are indebted to the official history of Carless, Capel & Leonard for information on how this came about.

Many years after the event, William Leonard wrote to Simms:

"It was in January 1893 when you came down to our works and we made an agreement to work together with regard to the sale of Launch Spirit for your Daimler launches that I said to you 'If we wish to keep the supply of spirit for your launches in our hands, it is absolutely necessary to give it a distinctive name.' We thought of several names, but you suggested it should be called Petrol. I objected to this at first because it was too like Petroleum, the trade name for paraffin oil, and was likely to be confused with it, but I finally accepted your suggestion and I drew up a pamphlet called the spirit we manufactured for your use in your launches Petrol and we have called it by that name ever since."

Thus, in adopting Simms' suggestion, Carless, Capel & Leonard gave a new word to the English language. Almost certainly too, they were the first refiners in Europe to make a petroleum product fully deodorised and doubly distilled of such light specific gravity on a commercial scale. Thus they can justly claim to be called the Pioneers of Petrol.

By May 1901, the company had embarked on a campaign to explain what petrol was. They published a brochure for distribution among the growing band of motorists, explaining the advantages of 'double distilled deodorised spirit', and listing the places where it might be obtained. Since today's tightly knit network of garages and filling stations was still some way off, the list included many ironmongers, chemists' shops and even private houses.

Until the infrastructure of petrol stations had been created, motorists making long journeys with their cars had to lay careful plans to ensure they would be able to obtain fuel. Sometimes they had even to wait until it arrived by train!. When Henry Sturmey, Editor of _The Autocar_, made his epic drive in a Coventry-built Daimler from John O'Groats to Lands End in 1898, he had to arrange fuel dumps along the route in advance, in much the same way that Scott and Amundsen had to do in their trek to the South Pole.

There was also a great deal of prejudice and ignorance about the new fuel. Regulations introduced in 1896 stipulated the need for extreme caution when dealing with petroleum. It might not be used, kept or conveyed in anything except closed unbreakable metal tanks. These tanks had also to be labelled with the words 'mineral spirit, highly inflammable, for use with light locomotives'. The amount of spirit allowed in petrol tanks was restricted, and tanks had to be filled away from artificial light. In those pre-electric light days, illumination of storage places posed quite a problem. Clearly gas and ordinary oil lamps were dangerous in confined places if leakages occurred.

Henry Sturmey arriving at Land's End at the finish of his epic drive from John O'Groats in 1898 in a Coventry-built Daimler. Crowds came out to see him along the way.

Once again Carless, Capel & Leonard came up with an answer after some careful research. Their booklet of 1899 draws attention to its Benzine Safety Lamps as *"Especially suitable for lighting coach houses where cars driven by petrol motors are kept."*

William Leonard was also instrumental in persuading the railways to introduce reasonable rates for the carriage of petrol. This was an important breakthrough in the establishment of an infrastructure for the distribution of petrol in Britain, since it enabled Carless, Capel & Leonard to make prompt deliveries to a network of suppliers around the country. Up until then, ironically in the dawning motor age, petrol was being delivered by horse-drawn vehicles!

The other aspect of the petroleum industry's importance to the world of motoring is lubrication. This is an area in which Charles Cheers Wakefield, later to become Viscount Wakefield and the founder of Castrol (now Burmah Castrol), played a vital role.

He started his business in 1899 in Cannon Street, London, selling oils for the lubrication of railway locomotives. In 1906 he began to sell Wakefield Motor Oil for the petrol engine. Later on this oil became known as Castrol, and the vegetable based Castrol R was to become a favourite of motor sporting enthusiasts, not least because of its aromatic properties when it burned in car engines.

With the growth of car ownership came a need to regulate the car, and to ensure

A Time of Change

PUNCH, OR THE LONDON CHARIVARI.—June 3, 1903.

THE RACE OF DEATH!

Some of the more humorous comments which appeared in 'Punch' and the 'Illustrated London News' before the passing of the Motor Car Act in 1903. The Act raised the speed limit from 12 mph to 20 mph. This seemed a huge increase at the time, although many cars were by then capable of speeds of 60 mph

"POLICEMEN ARE TO HAVE POWER TO PULL UP A MOTOR CAR AT ANY TIME

A Time of Change

Following a report in the 'Daily Telegraph' in September 1903 that Sir William Richmond R.A. had appealed to motor car manufacturers to produce something more beautiful than the existing monstrosities, these ideas appeared in 'Punch'. They were not so fanciful, since 'The Swan' was actually built for a Mr. Matthewson of Calcutta (below). 'The Autocar' reported that "the exhaust fumes exit by way of the nostrils, the eyes being formed of electric lamps".

THE SWAN

L'ART NOVEAU

THE CORNUCOPIA

THE CLASSIC

THE DOLPHIN

THE MEMPHIS.

E
OUIS
XIV.

THE ART AND CRAFTY.

69

A Time of Change

that it paid its way towards road building and road maintenance. After 1903 cars had to be registered with County Councils, and in 1909 a formalized system of vehicle tax was introduced, together with a tax on petrol. Police activity was a continual source of controversy, with speed traps proliferating. Constables were reported to hide in ditches to catch drivers, but no-one was quite sure how they managed to measure speeds. This led to the creation of the Automobile Association, whose Scouts used to warn drivers of an approaching police speed trap by failing to salute!

In that still Victorian age of 1899, the ground swell of the women's suffragette movement was just one further symptom of the speed of change at this time. The role of women in popularising the car was considerable. In August 1899, the *Daily Mail* reported under the headline 'The Autocar's Progress' that *"Lady automobilists are increasing rapidly. The longest run so far made by an English lady has been achieved by Mrs. Bazalgette who drove the other day from her house in Portman Square to Southampton."*

The close of the nineteenth century and the opening of the twentieth was thus a time of considerable change. The impact of the car on British society was making itself felt in all sorts of ways. It became linked to many other changes taking place at that time, and in its turn helped to accelerate the speed of change.

Pioneer woman motorist Mrs. Bazalgette won a silver medal for her part in the Thousand Mile Trial driving in a Benz car.

The Eclipse of the Crossing Sweeper

The Eclipse of the Crossing Sweeper

At a conservative estimate, there must have been some two million horses in London at the turn of the century. They were kept in livery stables and mews which are now the preserve of those who can still afford to live in the capital. The horses were fed from East Anglia, the granary of Britain, on fodder brought up London's river by Thames barges which would sail round from ports like Brightlingsea, Ipswich and Great Yarmouth. These barges were called Stackies, since they carried virtually whole haystacks on their decks. They travelled only when wind and tide would allow. In between tides, they would sit on the mud on their flat bottoms. It is worth noting that the coming of the internal combustion engine revolutionised the coastal shipping trade of this country. It also led to the extinction of the crossing sweeper.

It is common nowadays to criticise the motor vehicle's role in terms of atmospheric pollution of the environment. However, just what the pollution must have been like in a London populated by two million horses can perhaps best be left to the imagination. The crossing sweeper's job was to ensure that ladies could cross the street without getting the hems of their gowns horribly fouled. In return for a few coins, this man would make it possible for a pedestrian to proceed without offensive hindrance.

Ten years after having developed his first car, Daimler unveiled the first truck in 1896. In Germany, farmers were seen as prime potential customers for the new

Previous page: mixed horse-drawn and motorised traffic – the Mansion House in 1914.

The crossing sweeper (right) gradually disappeared from the London streets as the motor bus became more common.

mechanical replacement for the horse and cart. An early Daimler truck advertisement was clearly aimed at farmers, who might well have been expected to take a somewhat conservative view of the horseless waggon. The advertisement represented the vehicle as if it were an animal, since this was the best way to suggest that the substitution was sensible. The copywriter's line was:

"A Daimler is a good animal
It pulls like an ox as you can imagine
It doesn't feed while in the barn
And, drinks only when it works
It thrashes, saws and pumps as well
If you lack money, as is often the case
It is not affected by hoof and mouth disease
It doesn't play dumb tricks on you
It is not throwing you with its horns
It doesn't devour your good corn
For that reason, just through such
an animal
You will be well-provided for
for a long, long time.

History records that the first customer for this historic load-carrying successor to the horse and cart was the English Brewery of Samuel Allsop, now part of Allied Lyons. The new invention was soon to play an important part in the motorisation of public transport in Britain, as London and other cities turned increasingly towards motor buses. For many years these consisted of a Mercedes lorry chassis upon which British coachbuilders fitted double-deck bodywork.

In fact, the impact of the motor vehicle on the ordinary citizen of England during

An early Daimler lorry customer was Allsopp, the Burton brewery, now part of Allied Lyons.

73

The Eclipse of the Crossing Sweeper

the early days of this century was largely the result of the advent of the new motor bus. It was to be many years before cars would be cheap enough to be enjoyed by ordinary working people, through the efforts of British car makers such as Herbert Austin and William Morris. Internationally, the contributions of Henry Ford who introduced mass production as we understand it today and therefore paved the way for the affordable motor car, and Ferdinand Porsche, creator of the Volkswagen, also played a major role.

That famous judicial invention 'the man on top of a Clapham omnibus', created by a judge to represent the ordinary decent man in the street or reasonable man, who needed to be convinced in a legal dispute, would have been the first to experience the impact of the motor age on British society. It is interesting to speculate how it might have come about. The honest upright citizen of the early years of this century would probably have been going to work on a horse-drawn bus for much of his working life. He probably wore a blue serge suit, stiff collared shirt, and almost certainly had a bowler hat on his head. He would probably also sport a watch chain across his waistcoated chest.

Overnight he must have experienced the

Two paintings, 'St. Pancras Hotel from Pentonville Road' by J. O'Connor and 'Bayswater Omnibus' by G. W. Joy give a good impression of the age of the horse-drawn bus.

most dramatic change in his life. One day he was going to work on a horse-drawn bus, and the next he was part of the motor revolution, and was carried along on a vehicle which seemed to move of its own accord. The advantages of motorisation would not have been all that apparent at first. The new motor buses had to work themselves in for many years before they could be described as being as reliable as old Dobbin.

What the bowler-hatted ordinary citizen was experiencing was the almost imperceptible speeding up of the pace of life. Whether mankind as a whole would welcome this development, given the benefit of hindsight, is perhaps debatable. But there is no escaping the fact that the coming of the motor vehicle speeded life up, and the more leisurely pace of the nineteenth century gradually began to give place to the more frenetic pace of the twentieth century.

This time, it was another British entrep-

reneur who was to be charged with the task of importing Daimler's lorry chassis and putting them to work in the form of buses. He was George F. Milnes, and his company later came to be known as Milnes-Daimler and was to take over the car side as well.

Following the successes achieved in the Automobile Club's trials at Richmond in 1899, when the two- and five-ton Daimlers and the Daimler Waggonette all won medals, Milnes decided to tackle that bastion of steam engines – the Liverpool Self Propelled Traffic Association. Until 1901, the trials organised by this body were confined to steam driven vehicles. However, in 1901, two six horsepower lorries which had been brought into England from Cannstatt and Marienfelde by G. Milnes & Co. aroused considerable interest. This was the first time that internal combustion engines were pitted against steam. Their successes exceeded all expectations, and it was due largely to the victories they scored that commercial vehicles made by Daimler were to become so popular in England. *The Autocar* commented: *"Everyone was pleased with the excellent show the internal combustion engine machines made on their first appearance at the Liverpool trials."*

The delighted agent, George Milnes, reported to his suppliers in a letter dated London, 12th June 1901 :

"It is with considerable pleasure that we get to inform you that the two lorries which took part last week in the Liverpool Trials were awarded a Gold Medal and a Certificate; *the official numbers of the vehicles were AI and AII. From the beginning to the end of the trials, both vehicles met with the greatest success; no adjustments or repairs were required during the whole of the week of the trials during which time both vehicles were subjected to very severe usage.*

On the first day, when the hill-climbing tests were carried out, both vehicles had to climb gradients of 1 in 9, when empty and laden, and one of the vehicles while being driven at its normal speed of 8 mph, was stopped while going down this gradient in its own length. This was a very severe test for which we received congratulations from many quarters.

On the second day, the vehicles were driven from Liverpool to Manchester carrying a load of two tons – this was a run of some 41 miles. During the journey the fuel consumption amounted to 4½ gallons per vehicle at an average speed of 7½ mph.

On the third day, a return journey was made from Manchester to Liverpool, which proved equally successful. A similar load was carried and the utmost satisfaction was expressed at the success of this double trial. On the fourth and fifth days, a similar satisfactory journey was undertaken to Blackpool and back.

During all these tests, our vehicles were always in front so that a good average speed could be maintained without the necessity to hurry. On the sixth day, Saturday, 8th June, the vehicles were opened up so that the Judges could make the awards in the proper directions. Every part subject to wear and tear was on view, including the transmis-

sion, valves, differential gear and axles, etc., and although the vehicles, as mentioned already, had been subjected to extremely severe trials, and within four days had covered between 160 and 170 miles on the worst possible roads, no part showed the slightest signs of wear, and were apparently as good as new.

This is a highly satisfactory state of affairs both for you and us. Not only do we hope that this will lead to a largely increased sale of these vehicles, but their success may open up the question of whether you will be able to deliver fast enough to satisfy the many demands.”

There were still some problems ahead for the drive towards bringing public transport into the motor age. Just because the private car had reached a pinnacle of design in the Mercedes, it did not automatically follow that a satisfactory vehicle for large scale public transport would be produced by applying the Mercedes design principles. Vehicles had to carry fifty or more passengers, they had to be capable of stopping and restarting every few hundred yards, and furthermore, they had to cover vast distances every week under conditions much more severe than those applying to the ordinary private car. In other words, the demands of public transport were very different.

For this reason there were a number of false starts in the drive to motorise public transport in England. As early as 1902, the London Motor Omnibus Syndicate Ltd. was formed with a capital of only £3,000 in £1 shares. The idea was that a small fleet of so-called motor buses made by the Stirling Motor Carriage Co. should be put on London's streets. Within six months the firm went into liquidation. Another new company, also called the London Motor Omnibus Co. Ltd., was registered on 12th March 1903. Once again, it was a complete failure.

While these abortive attempts were being made to introduce the motor bus to London, the two principal caterers for public passenger service were experimenting in a small way with motor vehicles. They were the London General Omnibus Co. Ltd., and the London Road Car Company Ltd. Their experiences were not encouraging either. Solid tyres imposed tremendous stresses on the chassis frames, and no clutch had so far been devised which was capable of coping with the enormous strain of starting a heavy vehicle, carrying perhaps fifty passengers, every few hundred yards. Over-

One of the first British towns to adopt the motor bus in the form of a Milnes-Daimler was Hastings in 1904. By 1908, London also had Milnes-Daimler motor buses (see over).

77

The changing face of transport. Electric and steam power were both tried and found wanting. Although not immediately successful, the petrol-engined bus finally won through. Below: a 1908 poster advertising rides into the country by motor bus. Right top: a London steam bus of 1910 and below, steam buses at Witham, Essex, 1909. Opposite page, top right: an electric bus of 1896, and below, a 1908 Milnes-Daimler bus in London. Left: a 1914 Daimler motor bus undergoes the 'tilt-test'.

heating was common, and chassis frames began to sag in the middle. A few steam-engined buses were tried as well as 'petrol electric' in which the petrol engines were employed to top up the batteries which drove electric motors. But the results were not any better.

Then, at the beginning of 1905, a much more ambitious scheme was launched to put a large fleet of motor buses on London's streets. On 7th January a new company bearing the title of the London Motor Omnibus Company Ltd. was duly registered, and a public prospectus was issued inviting the public to take shares in the new venture. The nominal capital was £103,000 and an agreement had been formed between the new company and Milnes-Daimler Ltd. under which a fleet of Mercedes buses built by Daimler Motoren Gesellschaft would be imported. A number of such buses were already in use in Birmingham, Hastings, Eastbourne and Brighton, and it was anticipated that if each vehicle covered ninety miles per day, a net profit of 'at least 2d per mile' as the prospectus put it, would be earned. It was proposed to acquire seventy Mercedes motor buses in all, the original order being for twenty-five at a cost of £735.6s.8d. each. An agreement gave the London Motor Omnibus Company Ltd. the right to purchase a further seventy-five on the same terms within fifteen months. The contract also stipulated that Milnes-Daimler Ltd., and any purchaser of motor buses from them, should not ply for hire on certain routes listed in the agreement.

For the first few months, everything looked rosy. But ninety miles per day, week after week, was a very long distance for any heavy passenger-carrying vehicle conceived and built in 1905 to undertake. Breakdowns were frequent, the low tension magneto ignition began to give considerable trouble, and the thin solid rubber tyres were absolutely inadequate to absorb the road shocks and vibration. Overhauling and servicing left much to be desired, perhaps because people knew more about looking after horses than about looking after machines, and they simply had not caught up adequately with the new technology.

The ordinary man in the street could be forgiven for thinking, when the problem of the early motor bus impacted on his life, that he might have been better off if the horse had stayed around a bit longer. A particularly nasty accident to a chartered bus taking a party from London to Brighton also contributed to the poor image of the motor bus in its early days.

Even though the London Motor Omnibus Company Ltd. was voluntarily wound up in June 1907 with considerable loss of public money, the age of the motor bus had arrived. Motorised public transport did not fully take over from horses until much later, but its impact in the early 1900's was significant. Perhaps more than anything else, the motorisation of public transport paved the way for the subsequent success achieved by the internal combustion engine in Britain.

—The Power to Fly—

Above: Christian Lautenschlager, winner of the 1914 French Grand Prix. Previous page: Lautenschlager during the race.

This account of the motorisation of Britain nears to its close with one of the last images of peace before the first World War – a joint Anglo-German celebration of a hard-won victory in competitive motor sport.

When *"the lamps went out all over Europe,"* in Sir Edward Grey's immortal phrase, they were extinguished on a world which was never to be the same again. Followers of the popular television series *Upstairs Downstairs* will know that the war changed many things. It marked for example, the beginnings of a more responsible role for women in society, and a more egalitarian view of the place of the working man in the scheme of things.

The spreading influence of the motor car across international boundaries was also aided by the growing popularity of motor racing as a spectacle in the early part of the century. Just as Jellinek had demonstrated its value as a sales tool in 1901, so Daimler's heirs were also quick to grasp how racing successes in one country could be turned to advantage in others. This is clearly illustrated by a ruse they adopted in promoting their sensational victory in the French Grand Prix of 1914 at Lyon.

In that punishing seven-hour race, the Mercedes cars were initially given little chance against the favourite Peugeots, who were performing on their home ground. But led by Mercedes engineer Max Sailer (who also drove in the team), they managed to wear down the opposition with their sheer consistency, defeating thirty-two cars of a dozen different makes. The result was a 1-2-3 victory for the Mercedes team consisting of Lautenschlager, Wagner and Salzer.

After the race, the factory chiefs calmly painted Lautenschlager's winning No.28 on the radiators of all three cars, and despatched them to the three capitals whose opinions really counted in those days – London, Paris and Berlin. If anything, pre-World War I London was even more of an important centre for commerce than it is today.

London in August 1914 was hence the scene of a remarkable event - an Anglo-German celebration of the Mercedes 1-2-3 victory in the French Grand Prix of the previous month. The scene is London's fashionable Trocadero restaurant with its Palm Court atmosphere. The occasion was a dinner for the Press and VIP guests of the Milnes-Daimler Company. (By 1914 Milnes-Daimler had taken over responsibility not only for the importation of lorry chassis, but for the sale of Mercedes cars as well.)

We are indebted to *Car* magazine for permission to reproduce the following imaginative account of this occasion. It was stimulated by sight of the menu card, a copy of which passed through the hands of automotive historian David Burgess Wise on its way to the Daimler-Benz archives in Stuttgart:

"After dinner, Mr. Leslie Lambert (Prestidigitateur) will entertain ... along with Miss Lilian Burn (Mezzo Soprano), Mr. Walter Glynne (Tenor), and Mr. Astley Weaver

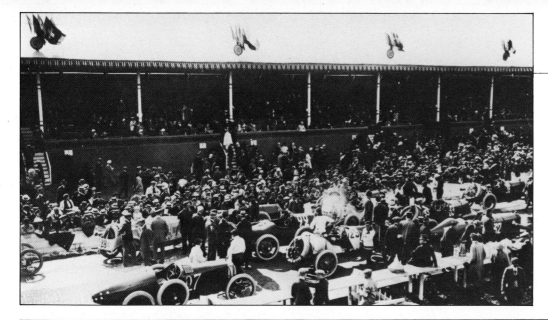

The Grand Prix, Lyon 1914. Left: scene at the start. Below: the Mercedes team who, in spite of early expectations of a French victory won the first three places: Christian Lautenschlager, Louis Wagner and Otto Salzer. The average speed during the race was 65.66 mph. The race was 468 miles long and lasted seven hours.

Lautenschlager

(Entertainer at the piano). Just two weeks short of the Great War, an Anglo-German company, uncomfortably hot in boiled shirts and dinner suits, suffered that indigestable post-prandial divertissement, puffing on their big Havana cigars amid the potted palms of the old Trocadero Restaurant in London. They had just waded through a massive ten-course meal to celebrate the Mercedes 1-2-3 victory in the 1914 French Grand Prix, their enjoyment surely tempered by the certain knowledge that their two nations were on the brink of war with each other.

The menu for this banquet was recently unearthed by Erik Johnson of Mercedes-Benz, and a real assault course for the digestion it must have been in those pre-Nouvelle Cuisine days, with the participants wading through such delights as Supreme de Sole Lautenschlager (in honour of the winning driver), Capon de Houdan Wagner (for the second place driver) and Selle d'Agneau de Galle Salzer (for number three). Further down the menu they could try Caneton d'Aylesbury a la Seiler (Hot Stuff) as some kind of mis-spelt tribute to Max Sailer who had led the 752 km race for the first five laps until a broken con-rod put him out of the running, but no-where was there any recognition of poor Pilette, fifth member of the Mercedes team who had started last and fought his way up through the field of thirty-seven starters into sixth place by the end of the first lap, and held seventh place for the next two laps before dropping out in the fourth.

Though 1-2-3 victories aren't especially uncommon these days, the French crowds had not seen anything quite like it before and watched in a stunned silence as the first Mercedes, driven by the moustachioed Christian Lautenschlager (who also won the 1908 French Grand Prix) roared over the line.

Despite the proximity of hostilities, the winning Mercedes was shown in the importers' showrooms in London's Long Acre, the remaining team cars, hastily repainted with Lautenschlager's race number '28' enabling the 'winning' car to appear simultaneously in Mercedes showrooms across Europe – not the last time such a ploy would be used by a motor manufacturer."

What happened next demonstrates the irony of the fortunes of war where advanced technology is concerned. On that fatal August Bank Holiday when war broke out, the Mercedes car was impounded by the British who were keenly aware that its overhead camshaft engine with welded on water-jacketed steel cylinders, was substantially the same as that used in German military aircraft. The engine provided much valuable information for Rolls Royce, who dismantled it to the last nut and bolt. The lessons this very advanced engine had to offer were soon incorporated into Rolls aero-engines which came into use in the later stages of the war.

Just as Daimler had been building aero engines at Cannstatt for several years, so Rolls were quick to diversify from motor cars into aero-engines. It is perhaps hardly surprising that the personalities

Tragically the victim of Britain's first aero accident, the Hon. C. S. Rolls (opposite) in his machine before his last fatal flight in July 1910. Rolls won the Gordon Bennett cup in 1905.

Below: the menu card for the victory banquet held at the Trocadero, Piccadilly after the French Grand Prix.

MERCÉDÈS GRAND PRIX TRIUMPH, 1914 OFFICIAL CELEBRATION

Banquet

Friday, July 17th, 1914

CHAIRMAN: E. KRAFTMEIER, ESQ.

TROCADERO RESTAURANT, LONDON, W.

involved with the novelty of the motor car were also fascinated by flight. For example the Hon C.S. Rolls, who started Rolls Royce, later lost his life in an aero accident; and the young Lord Brabazon of Tara, who was the first holder of a pilot's licence in Britain, had also taken part in early motor races such as the Gordon Bennett race in Ireland in 1903.

As cars continued to get faster and more reliable, their speed pushed back the frontiers of knowledge in a way which was of immense help to the early aviators. Just as the creation of the internal combustion engine paved the way for the Wright Brothers' epoch-making achievement at Kitty Hawk in 1903, so progress in car engineering continued to contribute to aviation for many years after. As early as 1909, Bleriot demonstrated the reliability of powered flight by crossing the English Channel. Progress also tends to speed up during a time of war, and it

was only 1919 when the Atlantic was conquered by a converted bomber.

The world was becoming a smaller place – thanks to the power to fly, which had been first envisioned by Gottlieb Daimler as long ago as 1888. That imperceptible speeding up of the pace of life, first noticed by the ordinary citizen on top of one of the early motor buses in the early 1900's, had accelerated to a remarkable degree by 1919 with Alcock and Brown's epic crossing of the Atlantic.

So in those years between 1886 and 1914, a remarkable revolution had been wrought. It shaped the world in which we live today. Insofar as the motorisation of Britain is concerned, it sprang from a chance meeting between two men who were to become firm friends. It was the friendship between Daimler and Simms which was the basis on which Britain entered the automotive age.

Pioneer motorist and aviator, Lord Brabazon of Tara (below) took part in the 1908 French Grand Prix in this 100 hp Austin car.

Right: Daimler supplied the 100 hp Mercedes aero-engine for this 1913 machine. Note the radiator under the wing.

Postscript

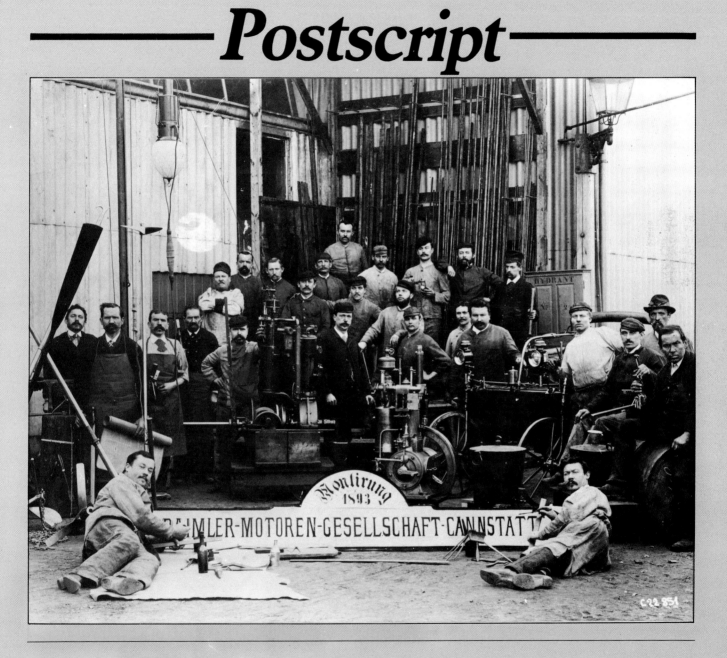

Postscript

In its short hundred years of life, the car has progressed from being a discovery, through a plaything of the rich, into an indispensable tool for mankind.

Given the choice, perhaps mankind might not have decided to accept the way of life that the car has made possible. However, there is no denying its enormous influence, not merely in terms of the quality of life, but also in the way it facilitates personal communications, goods distribution, shopping and leisure.

Even more significant, it is an important source of work for millions worldwide, not only in its manufacture, but also in servicing, selling, the exploration, gathering and distribution of oil, the building of roads, and administration of such matters as taxation and insurance.

Britain is a major vehicle manufacturing nation. The motor industry provides more jobs directly – over half a million – than any other manufacturing sector. It also contributes more wealth than any

other industry in terms of employment, value added, maintenance of a national technology base and foreign exchange earnings. As well as direct employment in manufacture, an estimated half-million Britons are employed in the motor trade and in the imported vehicle sectors.

An additional major contribution to employment is made by the road transport industry, which accounts for eight out of every ten tons of freight carried in Britain. The industry, upon which the country relies for the movement of almost all its goods, accounts for a further 400,000 jobs. Linked to all these direct activities are a myriad of supporting businesses, trade organisations, suppliers of goods and services.

In technological terms too, the business has advanced beyond all recognition from the cottage industry atmosphere in which it was first conceived. From the early experiments of Daimler and Maybach in the conservatory at Cannstatt, and Benz

Today in contrast, robots are used to do the final painting and to produce a high quality finish.

in Mannheim, the creation of today's and tomorrow's cars use mind-boggling techniques. The computer was called into play many years ago, and now uses its extraordinary abilities to process and sift through ideas and test them in simulation, far faster than mere humans could manage.

Once the shape of a new car has been determined and fashioned in clay by human hands, ultra-sensitive instruments 'read' the subtle shape in three-dimensional terms and store it in their electronic memories, so that it can be reproduced at will in flat, contoured drawings for the production engineer's use. The stresses and strains imposed by anticipated use – and even unimaginable abuse – are reproduced on individual components and whole structures in three dimensions on video screens by the computer. Thus countless years of highly skilled work and painstaking testing can be theoretically reproduced. The prudent manufacturer nevertheless still uses human brains and reactions in determining the final result.

An interesting example of how the modern Daimler-Benz Company uses this technology may be seen in their development of a special electronically equipped 'brake trailer' which, when towed behind a test car, reproduces the stresses and strains of mountain driving.

For many years, Daimler-Benz engineers used the Alpine passes of Southern Europe as a testing ground in the development of new models. The Gross-glockner pass in Austria was one of their favourites. But now, in the true 'Mountain to Mahomet' style, they have found a way to bring the mountain pass to their test track in Stuttgart. Through electronic data storage and sophisticated hydraulics, they can duplicate the same rolling resistance, wind resistance, acceleration resistance and climbing resistance encountered in hard driving in mountainous terrain. There is even a small engine in the trailer which counteracts the resistance generated by the trailer itself, thus ensuring accuracy to the nth degree.

In other ways too, the modern successors of Daimler and Benz still have their eyes firmly fixed on the future, and how to solve the problems it will bring. This is clear from the recent considerable emphasis given to the question of fuel conservation. Traditionally Daimler-Benz have been identified as makers of large, comfortable cars, able to cover long journeys easily. This is a type of car which might easily have been overwhelmed in a headlong rush towards the manufacture of smaller, more economical cars in the wake of the two energy shocks of the 1970's.

Daimler-Benz' answer was to accept the challenge of making the big car respectable. Firm in the belief that the future would still have a place for the car able to carry four or five people and their luggage swiftly over long distances, they embarked on a 'drying out' programme. Under the broad general title of 'The

When motoring started there were no garages as we know them today. Petrol was bought from chemists, ironmongers and even private houses. Above: an early garage of 1903, with Daimler cars in front. Motor agents repaired cycles too. Below: William Morris' garage and cycle shop in Longwall Street, Oxford, pictured in 1912, was the birthplace of one of Britain's best-known car companies.

Postscript

Energy Concept', Daimler-Benz engineers searched for ways of making their cars more economical without damaging their traditional high performance potential. To take just one example, they developed an automatic transmission which 'listens to the driver's foot.' This 'thinking' automatic transmission changes up early under normal driving conditions, but when the driver needs to accelerate smartly for any reason, sharp pressure on the accelerator pedal produces downchanges to give powerful acceleration on demand.

At the same time, keen scientific brains are looking even further ahead, towards a time when, many years from now, fossil fuel supplies may no longer be available. Engineers are studying measures to con-

serve existing resources, while at the same time exploring the possibilities offered by various alternatives. Thus Daimler-Benz is looking at a mixture of alternative energies and drive systems such as alcohol-based fuels like ethanol, ethanol-diesel emulsion, methanol and methanol mixed with petrol, hydrogen both pure and mixed with petrol, electro-propulsion, natural gas and gas turbine propulsion.

Clearly personal mobility, the gift of those early pioneers, will continue to play an important part in our lives for the forseeable future. People want to be mobile so as to be able to take advantage of job opportunities. They are prepared to make longer journeys to work so as to be able to enjoy a better quality of life than the crowded urban centres can offer. Leisure can also be expected to play an increasingly important role.

The business that began with two men working sixty miles apart at opposite ends of the Neckar Valley in Southern Germany one hundred years ago is today an industrial giant. Fortunately it has continued to attract forward-looking men, willing to devote themselves to the task of producing cars which are fast enough, safe enough and economical enough to meet future needs. Not to mention clean enough to avoid irreparable damage to the environment. For them, and for the future generations of motor industry engineers, Daimler's motto is still as eloquent as it ever was:

Nothing but the Best

Below: Early advertisements for tyres. Roads had to be improved to withstand the pressure of car tyres.

Right: in 1901 an early attempt was made to market a 'small' Mercedes in Britain. However, the large 35 hp car overshadowed it. Recently, a new smaller series of saloon cars – the 190 range – became an international success.

EARLY MOTOR CAR TYPES.

No. 5.—The Gladiator.

The year 1896, marked in the Dunlop Series by an early Gladiator car, was an eventful one in the history of motoring. On November 13th to drive without being preceded by a man carrying a red flag, or without complying with the law laid down for the regulation of traction engines and steam rollers, was to pursue the direct road to the police station. A day later this anomaly was removed, and motor cars were allowed to pursue peacefully the path of evolution, though at the strictly limited speed of 12 miles per hour. Emancipation Day, as November 14th was dubbed, was celebrated by a drive to Brighton, in which 33 cars took part, 13 surviving the journey.

The illustration is interesting also in that it shows a type of vehicle that has now almost disappeared from the London streets. One may safely prophesy that to the next generation the horse-drawn omnibus will be known only by pictorial representation. Such a thought, one may be sure, never entered the heads of the "outsides" as they gazed with amusement on the little Gladiator alongside in 1896.

In tyre history, too, 1896 has a special significance. It was the first year in which Dunlops came into general use for motor cars, and from that year onwards there has been a steady rise in both Dunlop quality and reliability, until, like the modern car, it is difficult to see in what way they can be improved.

DUNLOP
TYRES

FIRST IN 1888; FOREMOST EVER SINCE.

The Dunlop Rubber Co., Ltd., Aston Cross, Birmingham; and 14, Regent Street, London, S.W.

Paris: 4, Rue du Colonel Moll.

Berlin: S.W. 13, Alexandrinenstrasse, 110.

1896

JOHN BULL
BRITAIN'S BEST
TYRES

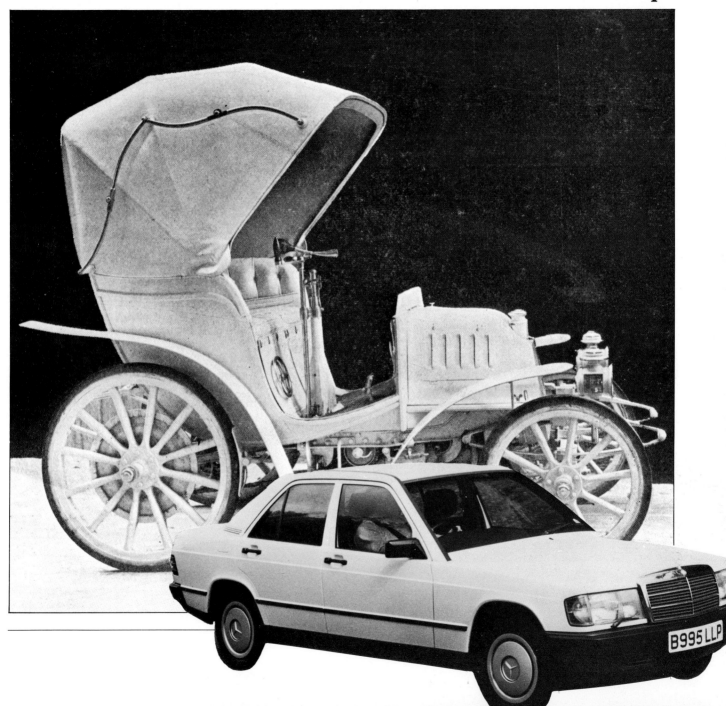

INDEX

PHOTOGRAPHIC ACKNOWLEDGEMENTS

Carless, Capel & Leonard 64
Castle Museum, York 3
Daimler-Benz Archive, 7, 8, 9, 11, 12,
    13, 15, 17, 18, 20, 21, 22, 23, 25,
    26, 28, 35, 40, 41, 42, 43, 44, 45,
    51, 52, 58, 73, 82, 85, 86, 87, 88,
    89, 93
John Freeman 12, 27, 28, 30, 37, 39, 44,
    45, 47, 53, 56, 60, 66, 67, 68-9, 84
London transport Executive 71, 78
Mansell Collection 6, 33, 38, 40, 54, 58,
    92
Museum of London 72, 74, 75
National Motor Museum 27, 30, 32, 33,
    45, 47, 51, 53, 54, 55, 70, 77, 78,
    79, 81, 83, 86, 91, 92
National Trust 19
Roger-Viollet 48
Science Museum 10, 49, 50
Eileen Tweedy 14, 59, 61
Victoria and Albert Museum 16

Opposite page: Poster drawing, 1985 by
    Gi Neuert.

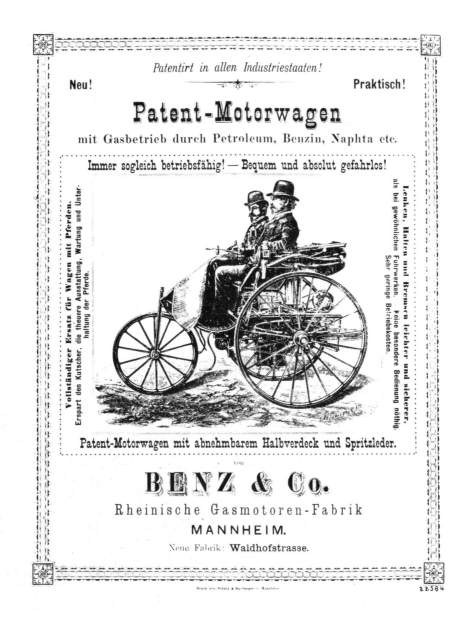